THE ORIGIN
OF THE
BENGALI SCRIPT

PLATE I.

Fragmentary Inscription on image of Budha-Rajgir-Patna (I. M.) No. N. S. 2.

THE ORIGIN
OF THE
BENGALI SCRIPT

BY

R. D. BANERJI

ISBN : 978-93-5324-549-8 (HB)

First Published, Calcutta, 1919

Published, 2020

Published by

Facsimile Publisher
12 Pragati Market
Ashok Vihar, Ph-2
Delhi-110052
E-mail: books@facsimilepublisher.com

Printed at: G. Print Process, Delhi.

The Origin of the Bengali Script

Author: R. D. Banerji

THE ORIGIN

OF THE

BENGALI SCRIPT

BY

R. D. BANERJI, M.A.

PUBLISHED BY THE

UNIVERSITY OF CALCUTTA

1919

To my Teachers

of

Indian Palæography

The Late Dr. Theodor Bloch, Ph.D.,

and

Mahamahopadhyaya Hara Prasad Sastri,
M.A., C.I.E.

PREFACE

This essay on the origin of the Bengali Script was originally written by me in my mother tongue at the suggestion of the late Āchārya Rāmendra Sundara Trivedī, Principal of the Ripon College, who to my great regret has not lived to see its publication. Principal Trivedi intended to publish this essay in the Journal of the Baṅgīya Sāhitya Pariṣad, of which learned Society he was the Secretary and one of the founders. At the suggestion of the Hon'ble Justice Sir Āśutoṣa Mukhopādhyāya, Sarasvatī, Śāstra-Vāchaspati, it was translated into English and submitted with Principal Trivedī's consent for the University of Calcutta Jubilee Research Prize which was awarded to me in 1913. The publication of this work was undertaken by the University of Calcutta at the direction of the Hon'ble Justice Sir Āśutoṣa Mukhopādhyāya, Sarasvatī, Śāstra-Vāchaspati, Kt., C.S.I., M.A., D.L., Ph.D., D.Sc., etc., then Vice-Chancellor of the University.

I am indebted to my teacher the venerable Pandit Mahāmahopādhyāya Hara Prasāda Śāstrī, M.A., C.I.E., formerly Principal of the Government Sanskrit College, Calcutta, and now President of the Asiatic Society of Bengal, and Dr. D. B. Spooner, B.A., Ph.D., F.A.S.B., formerly Superintendent, Archæological Survey, Eastern Circle, and now Officiating Director General of Archæology in India, for many corrections and valuable suggestions. My friend Mr. Surendranath Kumar has helped me greatly by translating portions of works in German and French for my use. My pupil Prof. Kalidas Nag, M.A., of the Scottish Churches College, Calcutta, has revised the type-written manuscript twice and has corrected many of the proofs. My thanks are due to Sj. Hemchandra Gosvāmī, Extra Assistant Commissioner, Gauhati, Assam, for pointing out the modern Bengali inscription recording the dedication of the image of Āmrātakeśvara at Kāmākhyā near Gauhati in Assam. To my friend Pandit Vasanta Rañjana Rāya Vidvadvallabha Kavirañjana, the Custodian of the manuscript collection of the Baṅgīya Sāhitya Pariṣad, I owe a deep debt of gratitude. Mr. Rāya has enabled me to complete the history of the development of the Bengali Script by collecting transitional and final forms from the manuscript of Caṇḍidāsa's Kṛṣṇa Kīrttana, discovered by him in Bankura, a task which I could never have succeeded in completing without his aid. I am indebted to the Council of the Asiatic Society of Bengal and the Executive Committee of the Baṅgīya Sāhitya Pariṣad for permission to photograph and reproduce certain pages of a manuscript of the Bodhicharyāvatāra of Śāntideva, written in 1492 V. E., and of the Kṛṣṇa-Kīrttana of Caṇḍīdāsa.

POONA,
20th August, 1919.

CONTENTS

LIST OF ILLUSTRATIONS

CHAPTER I

INTRODUCTION

A. The arrangement.

In an essay on the origin and development of the Bengali script, one must necessarily follow the steps of the late Hofrath Dr. Georg Bühler, the father of the science of Indian Palæography. Though Burnell's work on the subject was published long ago, the accuracy of the narrative and the scientific arrangement of Bühler's work have made his claim to the title indisputable. His *Indische Palaeographie* was published in 1896, as a part of the *Grundriss der indo-arischen Philologie und Altertumskunde*, organised by that indefatigable publisher, Dr. Karl J. Trübner of Strassburg. The work, as a matter of course, was short and concise, and dealt with the development of Indian alphabets up to the 12th century A. D. The development of the alphabets, from B. C. 350 to 600 A. D., is clearly described in this work. But after that period, lack of materials obliged the learned author to consider the development of the Northern alphabet as a whole, and not according to its varieties. The discoveries made during the last sixteen years have rendered it possible to take up that work now. The arrangement followed in these pages is mainly that of Dr. Bühler's from the dawn of the historical period to the 6th century A. D., but is different with regard to the subsequent periods. In latter periods, more attention has been paid to specimens from North-Eastern India, and the latest discoveries added to the list of epigraphs, have been analysed. Thus, the inscriptions on the railing-pillars at Bodh-Gayā have been placed in their proper position in the chronological order according to the new light thrown on them. In the Gupta period, the addition of a new variety of the alphabet is now possible, owing to the discoveries of the remains of ancient Indian civilisation in the deserts of Central Asia. Fresh discoveries have also made it possible to trace the gradual displacement of the Eastern variety of the Northern alphabet by the Western one, in the 5th and 6th centuries A. D., and to determine the exact epoch of the final displacement. Finally, new materials have facilitated the determination of the type specimens of each variety, in each particular century, with a nearer approach to accuracy.

From the 7th century onward, it has been found impossible to follow the arrangement in Dr. Bühler's work, as the development of the Eastern variety from 600-1100 A. D. has not been clearly shown there. In the following pages, the alphabets of the North-Eastern inscriptions of the 6th and 7th centuries A.D. have been separately analysed. In the 8th century, we find three different varieties of the alphabet in Northern India, or more strictly four, if we count the alphabet of Afghanistan, which is as yet but little known The Western and Afghanistan varieties were developed from the old Western variety, while the Central and Eastern varieties were evolved out of the old Eastern. The Eastern variety lost ground and its Western boundary gradually receded eastwards. The development, of the Eastern alphabet only, has been followed in these pages. It has become possible to show, that proto-Bengali forms were evolved in the North-East, long before the invasion of Northern India, by the Nāgarī alphabet of the South-West, and that Nāgarī has had very little influence upon the development of the Bengali script. The chronology of the Pāla dynasty of Bengal, and specially their relations with the Gurjjara-Pratīhāras have been settled from synchronisms, and a detailed discussion of the subject will be found in my monograph on the *Pālas of Bengal* [1]

It is evident that Nārāyaṇapāla preceded Mahendrapāla and Magadha, specially the Western portion of it was included for sometime in the Empire of the Gurjjara-Pratīhāras. The establishment of this sequence is of the utmost importance, as it enables us to treat the analysis of Pāla records, which are dated in the majority of cases in regnal years, with more confidence.

With the introduction of the Nāgarī script in the 10th century, the Western limit of the use of the Eastern alphabet was still further reduced. In the 11th century, we find that, there is very little similarity between the alphabet used in Benares and that used in Gayā. The progress of the changes has been very rapid, and we find the complete proto-Bengali alphabet in the 11th century A.D. In the 12th century, we find further changes, which make the formation of the modern Bengali alphabet almost complete. The final development of certain letters, such as *i*, *ca* and *ṇa*, are not noticeable until after the Muhammadan conquest. The dearth of records of the 13th and 14th centuries A.D., both manuscript and epigraphic, makes it impossible to follow the development of these letters in this period. The shock of the Muhammedan conquest paralysed Eastern India, from which it never recovered entirely. The blow stunned literature, prevented its growth during the first two centuries after the conquest, and a partial revival was made only in the 15th century. The revival received a fresh impetus from the Neo-Vaiṣṇavism of Caitanya and his followers. With the paralysis of literature, the development of the alphabet also stopped. Very few

---

[1] Memoirs of the Asiatic Society of Bengal, Vol. V, Pt. III,

changes have, indeed, been made in the Eastern alphabet from the 12th century A.D. down to the nineteenth. Such changes, as are noticeable, were made during the 15th and 16th centuries, and have been illustrated by the alphabet used in two Mss. written in Bengali :—

(1) Śāntideva's *Bodhicaryāvatāra,* copied in Vikrama Samvat 1492 (1435 A.D.), discovered by Mahāmahopādhyāya Haraprasāda Śāstrī, C. I. E., in Nepal and purchased by him for the Asiatic Society of Bengal. (No. *G.* 8067.) The complete colophon of this ms. has already been published by me in my monograph on Saptagrāma.[1]

(2) Caṇḍīdāsa's *Kṛṣṇa-Kīrttana,* a new work discovered by Paṇdit Vasantarañjana Rāya, Vidvadvallabha, the Keeper of the ms. collection of the Vaṅgīya-Sāhitya-Pariṣad. Though the material is paper, the script makes it impossible to assign the ms. to any date later than the 14th century A.D.

The completely developed alphabet has not changed at all during the 17th and 18th centuries A.D. In the 19th century, the vernacular and classical literature received a fresh impetus, as the result of the contact with the West, but the alphabet ceased to change. Its forms were stereotyped by the introduction of the printing press, and it is not likely that in future it will change its forms in each century.

B. The limits of the use of the Eastern Variety.

From the beginning of the Empire of the Mauryas till the downfall of the Imperial Guptas, Allahabad and its immediate neighbourhood formed the western limit of the use of the Gupta alphabet. The western

---

[1] J. A. S. B. (N. S.), Vol. V, p. 253.

limit is the most important one, as this was the only limit which changed its position. Upon the formation of a Western variety in the North-Eastern alphabet, this limit gradually receded eastwards. In the 3th century, Benares formed the eastern boundary of the Western variety, but in the beginning of the 11th century, we find that the limit has receded further East. In the 12th century, both varieties were being used in Magadha, as is shown by the Govindapur Stone Inscription of the Śaka year 1059,[1] and the Bodh-Gayā Inscription of Jayaccandra.[2] After the Muhammadan conquest, the Western variety gradually spread itself over the whole of South Bihār or Magadha, and the use of the Eastern variety was confined to the western limits of Bengal proper. The use of the Eastern variety, however, lasted in Magadha till the 14th century, when we find it in votive inscriptions, on flag-stones in the court-yard of the Great Temple at Bodh-Gayā,[3] and in a new inscription discovered by Mr. Lāl Bihāri Lāl Singh, Deputy Superintendent of Police, Bihār. The Gayā-*Prapitāmaheśvara* temple inscription of V. S. 1257 and the Umgā Hill inscription of Bhairavendra[4] (V. S. 1496 = 1439 A.D.) show that Nāgarī had entirely displaced the Eastern variety in Magadha.

In the north the snowy mountains formed the northern limit. But in the north-east the Bengali alphabet was adopted in Assam, where not only in the Kamauli grant of Vaidyadeva, but also in other inscriptions, Bengali characters have been exclusively

---

[1] Epigraphia Indica, Vol. II, p. 333.

[2] Memoirs, A. S. B., Vol. V, pl. xxxv.

[3] Cunningham's Archæological Survey Reports, Vol. I, Pl. II, Nos. 1 & 2.

[4] J. A. S. B. (N. S.), Vol. II, p. 29.

used. In the Assam plates of Vallabhadeva of the Saka year 1107 = 1185 A.D.[1] we find archaisms, which lurked in the backwoods of civilisation. In the east the Bengali script was also being used in Sylhet, where similar archaisms are to be met with in the Sylhet grants of Keśavadeva [2] and Īśānadeva.[3] In the south the Bengali script was used throughout Orissa. We find the proto-Bengali script in the Ananta Vāsudeva temple inscription of Bhaṭṭa Bhavadeva at Bhuvaneśvara, and the modern Bengali alphabet in the grants of the Gāṅga Kings Nṛsiṁhadeva II [4] and Nṛsiṁhadeva IV. [5] The modern cursive Oḍiyā script was developed out of the Bengali after the 14th century A. D. like the modern Assamese.

---

[1] Epigraphia Indica, Vol. V, p. 183.

[2] Proceedings, A. S. B., 1880, p. 148.

[3] *Ibid*, p. 152.

[4] J. A. S. B., 1896, Pt. I, p. 235.

[5] *Ibid*, 1895, Pt. I, p. 136.

CHAPTER II

The Northern Indian Alphabets (B.C. 350—A.D. 600).

A. The Older Maurya Alphabet.

Leaving aside the various theories about the origin of the ancient Indian alphabet, we turn to examine it as it has been found to exist at the beginning of the historical period. It is sufficient for the purpose of the present article that Dr. Bühler recognised the antiquity of the Indian Alphabet in Aśoka's time. "The existence of so many local varieties, and of so very numerous cursive forms, proves, in any case, that writing had had a long history in Aśoka's time and the alphabet was then in a state of transition." [1] The alphabet is also recognised to be "a script framed by learned Brāhmans for writing Sanskrit."[2] The earliest Indian inscription is the record on the Piprāwā vase discovered in 1898. It can be proved on palæographical grounds that the forms of Brāhmī letters used in incising this record are older than those of Aśoka's inscriptions. The vases found in the Stūpa at Piprāwā contained according to one authority the relic (*Śarīra*) of Buddha himself,[3] and according to another, those of his kinsmen of the Śākya clan.[4] It has been surmised that the stūpa was raised over the relics of the Śākyas, who were slain by Viruḍhaka, King of Kośala, during the life-time of Buddha

---

[1] Bühler's Indian Palæography (Eng. Ed.), p. 7.

[2] *Ibid*, p. 17.

[3] J. R. A. S., 1898, p. 388.

[4] J. R. A. S., 1905, p. 680.

himself. Consequently the date of the Piprāwā inscription must lie either in the 5th or the 4th centuries B.C. Palæographical evidence fully supports this conclusion: the archaic forms of the Brāhmī alphabet found on the Persian *sigloi*, which went out of the general use in Aśoka's time, are found to have been used in the inscription. An analysis, of the characters of this inscription, would be out of place here, as it does not properly belong to the Eastern variety of the Maurya alphabet. It serves to indicate the upper limit of the use of the alphabet of this period. The lower limit has been fixed by Bühler at 200 B. C.[1] The seals, found by Cunningham at Pātnā,[2] which according to Bühler belong to the period when Brāhmī was written boushophedon (βουστροφπδον), were really seal-matrices, like the Rohṭāsgaḍh Rock seal-matrix of the *Mahāsāmantādhipati* Śaśāṅka.[3]

B. Varieties of the Older Maurya Alphabet.

In 1896, Bühler admitted the existence of two distinct varieties of this alphabet, *viz* :—

(*i*) the Northern : to be found in the rock-edicts at Kālsi, the pillar-edicts at Allahabad, Rādhiā, Māthiā, Niglivā, Paḍeriā and Rāmpurwā, the minor rock-edicts at Bairāṭ, Sahasrām, the inscriptions of the Barābār caves and Sāñci and Sārnāth pillars ;

(*ii*) the Southern : to be found in the-rock edicts at Girnār, Dhauli and Jaugaḍa and the minor rock-edicts at Siddapura.

Bühler already noticed the existence of varieties, at this period, in the Northern Maurya alphabet. "Even

[1] Indian Palæography (Eng. Ed.), p. 33.

[2] Cunningham's Arch. Survey Report, Vol. XV, Pl. III.

[3] Fleet's Gupta Inscriptions, p. 283, Pl. xliii B.

the writings in the northern versions are not quite homogeneous. The pillar edicts of Allahabad, Mathia, Nigliva, Paḍeria, Radhia and Rampurwa form a very closely connected set, in which only occasionally minute differences can be traced, and the edicts of Bairāṭ No. I, Sahasram, Barabar and Sāñci, do not differ much. A little further off stands the Dhauli separate edicts (where Edict VII has been written by a different hand from the rest), the Delhi-Mirāṭ edicts and the Allahabad Queen's edict, as these show the angular *da*. Very peculiar and altogether different is the writing of the rock-edict of Kālsi, with it, some letters on the coins of Agathocles and Pautaleon (but also some in the Jaugaḍa separate edicts), agree. Perhaps, it is possible to speak also of a North-Western variety of the older Maurya alphabet."[1]

Thus Bühler distinguishes three different sub-varieties in the Northern Maurya alphabet. According to their geographical distribution, they may be classified as follows :—

(*a*) The North-Eastern—found in the Allahabad, Rādhiā, Māthiā, Rāmpurwā, Niglivā, Paḍeria and the Sārnāth pillar edicts. The Earthen seals found at Pātnā[2] (seal matrices bearing the inverted inscriptions *Naṁdāya* and *Agapalasa*) as well as that found by Cunningham at Bodh-Gayā[3] (*Mokhalinam*) belong to this period.

(*b*) The North-Central—found in the rock-edicts at Bairāṭ and Sahasrām, the pillar-edicts at Sāñci and Delhi and the cave-inscriptions at Barābār.

---

[1] *Ibid*, p. 34.
[2] Cunningham's Archæological Survey Rep., Vol. XV, Pl. III. 1, 2.
[3] Cunningham's Mahabodhi, Pl. XXIV, p. 1.

(*c*) The North-Western—represented by the characters of the Kālsi rock-edicts and the letters on the coins of the Greek kings Agathocles and Pantaleon.

In this paper we are concerned only with the North-Eastern variety, of the older Maurya-alphabet, and such inscriptions of the Northern Central variety as are to be found in North-Eastern India. A detailed description of the older Maurya alphabet would also be out of place here, as it is not yet possible to improve upon Dr. Bühler's admirable description of it. Consequently, one has to remain content, simply with the noting of the peculiarities of the alphabet as found in different inscriptions. Among vowel signs the only letter to be noted is the initial *ī* which has been found in one of the inscriptions on the railings around the great temple at Bodh-Gayā, where Bühler reads *Īdāgimitasa* for *Iṁdāgimitasa* read by Cunningham.[1] But in reality, the characters of this inscription belong to the younger Maurya alphabet, as shown by Bloch. Among the consonants the form of *kha* found in one of the inscriptions at Bodh-Gayā,[2] with a triangle as its base, should be noted, but this inscription also, belongs to the younger Maurya alphabet. The only instance of *ṇa*, among the inscriptions of this period, is to be found in the mason's marks on the pillars of Buddha's walk, inside the temple enclosure at Bodh-Gayā. *Cha* with two loops, one on each side of a vertical straight line, instead of a circle divided into two unequal parts, have also been found among the mason's marks on the pillar-bases of Buddha's walk. The usual form of *ja*, is the Northern form with a loop or a dot. Other letters do not call for special attention but forms of the test letters *ya*, *la*, *sa* and *ha* may be noted. The form of *ya* is essentially the Northern one, which Bühler calls

---

[1] Mahābodhi, Pl. X, Nos. 9 and 10.

[2] *Ibid*, Pl. X, No. 5.

the "notched *ya*." The form of *la* is generally cursive. One important exception is to be found, in the extremely cursive form, used in the Jaugaḍa separate edicts, which is essentially the same to be found in the Eastern variety of the Early Gupta alphabet of the 4th and 5th centuries A.D. The position of the Jaugaḍa edict is somewhat peculiar. The edicts of Dhauli and Jaugaḍa, though relegated to the Southern variety of the older Maurya alphabet, stand in an intermediate position. "The Southern variety is most strongly expressed in the Girnār and Siddapura edicts, less clearly in the Dhauli and Jaugaḍa edicts by differences in the signs for *a*, *ā*, *kha*, *ja*, *ma*, *ra*, *sa*, the medial *i*, and the ligatures with *ra*."[1] Most probably, the cursive forms of *ha* and *la*, found in the Jaugaḍa separate edicts, were imported from Northern India, as will be seen later on. In the North-Eastern variety, the usual form of *ha* is also cursive. The extremely cursive form of this letter, in the Jaugaḍa separate edicts, is peculiar and an importation from the North.[2] This statement is corroborated by the discovery of a slightly different cursive form in the Allahabad separate edicts, line 1 in the word *mahāmāta*.

C. *The Younger Maurya Alphabet.*

The last eight columns, of Plate II of Bühler's tables, represent the younger Brāhmī alphabet of Northern India. The letters are taken from six series of inscriptions—

(*i*) The Nāgārjunī cave-inscriptions of Daśaratha, *ca.* 200 B.C.

(*ii*) The inscriptions on the *Toraṇas*, railing-pillars and cross-bars of the Bhārhut Stūpa, *ca.* 150 B.C.

---

[1] Ind. Palæo. (Eng. Ed.), p. 34.

[2] Burgess, Stūpa of Amarāvatī, p. 125.

(*iii*) The cave inscriptions at Pabhosa in the United Provinces, *ca*. 150 B.C.

(*iv*) The oldest inscriptions from Mathurā. These letters are principally taken from the oldest inscriptions discovered by Dr. A. Führer during the excavations at *Kaṅkālī Ṭīlā*, but the most ancient inscription from the district of Mathurā was discovered by Cunningham at Parkham. This inscription is incised on the base of a mutilated image of Yakṣa, at present in the Archæological Museum at Mathurā[1]. Most probably its characters belong to the younger Maurya alphabet.

(*v*) The Hāthigumphā inscription of Khāravela of Kaliṅga, *ca*. 160 B. C.

(*vi*) The Nānāghāṭ inscriptions of the Andhras, *ca*. 150 B. C.

Among these, only the Nāgārjunī cave-inscriptions of Daśaratha can be said to belong to the North Eastern variety. During subsequent years one other group has been added to the above list :

(*vii*) The inscriptions on the railing-pillars around the great temple at Bodh-Gayā. The late Dr. Theodor Bloch drew attention to the fact that "the older part of the Bodh-Gayā railing was put up in the middle of the 2nd century B. C., about 100 years after the time of Aśoka".[2] The cave-inscriptions of Daśaratha are about half a century older than those on the railing pillars at Bodh-Gayā. The following points are worth noting on the alphabet of the cave inscriptions :—

(1) the form of *la* closely resembles, that of the extremely cursive one, found in the Jaugaḍa separate edicts (see *ante* p. 14);

---

[1] Cunningham, A. S. R., Vol. XX, p. 41, Pl. VI. ; Vogel, Cat. of Arch. Museum at Mathurā, 1910, p. 83, C. I.

[2] Annual Rep. Arch. Surve yof India, 1908-9, p. 147.

PLATE II.

Fragmentary Kusana Inscription-Rajgir-Patna (I. M. No. 6283).

(2) the form of lingual *ṣa* is peculiar and resembles the form found in the Kālsi edicts, probably, it was the precursor of the looped lingual *ṣa* found in Eastern India in the 4th or 5th centuries A.D.;

(3) the form of *ha* is primitive and resembles that of the Siddapura edicts;[2]

(4) the form of *ṣa* shows an advance—the upper hook has been lengthened to form a slightly slanting second horizontal line.

The form of the remaining letters in Column XVII of Plate II of Bühler's work does not call for remarks. The inscriptions on the railing-pillars and cross-bars at Bodh-Gayā exhibit further changes, though they were incised only about fifty years after Daśaratha's time :—

(*a*) *a* shows two forms. In the word *Amoghasa* the first letter is decidedly of southern appearance[1] (*e.g.* Pl. II, Col. VIII, 1.); the other form is to be found in the various inscriptions of the noble lady *Kuraṅgi* and resembles that used in the Hāthigumphā inscriptions (Pl. II, Col. XXI, 1);

(*b*) *ka* has invariably the dagger-shaped form which was current up to the end of the 6th century A.D. and was formed by the elongation of the vertical line of the older Maurya form, cf. *ka* in *Tabapanaka*[2], *Kuraṅgiye* , *Sakaputrasa*[4], *Cetika*[5];

(*c*) *kha* occurs once only, in *Bodhirakhitasa*[6] where it resembles the form used in the oldest inscription in Mathurā (Pl. II, Col. XX, 10); there is a very slight difference between these two forms, the Eastern variety form as found in the Bodh-Gayā inscription, being slightly longer than that of the Western variety;

---

[1] Bühler's Indian Palæography, p. 36. [4] *Ibid*, Pl. X, 4—7, 9—10.

[2] Cunningham's Mahābodhi, Pl. X, 2. [3] *Ibid*, Pl. X, 3.

[5] *Itid*, Pl. X, 10. [6] *Ibid*, Pl. X, 9, 10. [7] *Ibid*, Pl. X, 3.

(*d*) *ga* occurs several times in the name *Kuraṅgi*[1] where it has two varieties :—(1) cursive as in Pl. X, p. 4 and (2) the angular as in Pl. X, 6-7 ;

(*e*) *gha* also occurs only once in *Amoghasa*[2] ; its appearance shows great change, though it resembles one of the forms used in the Kālsi edicts (Pl. II, Col. 3-12) ; it is, on the whole, different from the form to be found in the North-Eastern variety of the early Maurya alphabet;

(*f*) *ca* occurs twice in *Cetika*,[3] but its form does not show much difference from that of the older Maurya one;

(*g*) two forms of *ja* are to be found in these inscriptions:—(*i*) one form resembles the *ja* in Bühler's Pl. II, Col. X, 15, while (*ii*) the other form is the usual older Maurya one with a dot in place of the central loop;

(*h*) *ta* resembles the southern form in Bühler's Pl. II, Col. VII, 23 and the usual form of later Brāhmī inscriptions;

(*i*) *da* occurs in all of the inscriptions discovered on the pillars, copings and cross-bars of the Bodh-Gayā railing, and resembles the angular form of the older Maurya alphabet (Bühler Pl. II, Col. V-VI, 23);

(*j*) *dha* occurs once only in *Bodhirakhitasa*; there is no change in the form of this letter from the 3rd century B.C. till the 10th or 11th century A. D.;

(*k*) *na* also occurs in all of the inscriptions from Bodh-Gayā and its base line shows no curvature at all, proving that these inscriptions cannot be placed later than the 2nd century B. C.;

(*l*) *pa* shows a greater degree of change; in all cases of its occurrence, it shows two well-formed right angles, at its lower extremeties; cf. *Tabapanakasa*,[4] *Sakaputrasa*, *Jivāputrāye*,[5] *Pājāvātiye*, *Jivāputrāye* and *Pāsādā*[6].

---

[1] *Ibid*, Pl. X, 4—7, 9—10.

[2] *Ibid*, Pl. X, 2.

[3] *Ibid*, Pl. X, 9, 10.

[4] *Ibid*, Pl. X, 3.

[5] *Ibid*, Pl. X, 9.

[6] *Ibid*, Pl. X, 10.

(*m*) the form of *ba* shows no change;

(*n*) two forms of *ma* have been found in these inscriptions :—(1) *ma* with a circle at the lower part and a semicircle over it, as in *Amoghasa*[1] and (2) *ma* with a triangle at the lower part and a right angle over it, as in *Mitrasa*[2];

(*o*) two forms of *pa* also are to be found: the first form is the notched one, which is to be found on the coping inscriptions only,[3] and the second form, that with the curve below, is to be found in pillar-inscriptions[4];

(*p*) *ra* is always represented by a curved line;

(*q*) *va* shows the formation of a triangle at its base in the place of the circle;

(*r*) two forms of the dental *sa* are to be found: on one of the inscribed cross-bars, we find a slight curve to the left, attached to the lower extremity of the lower hook, cf. *sa* in *Amoghasa*; the other form is the usual older Maurya one, where in some cases, the elongation of the lower hook, marks a slight modification;

(*s*) *ha* has been found only once in the inscription recently discovered by the late Dr. Bloch, where it occurs in a ligature. The form of this letter, in the word *Brahmamitra*[5] is extremely cursive and shows that this hooked form is peculiar to the eastern variety of the older alphabets of Northern India;

(*t*) The newly discovered inscription has supplied a new letter *ña* which is to be found in the first word in *rāño*, and resembles the form in the Bhārhut and the Pabhosa alphabets with a downward elongation of the left vertical line.

---

[1] *Ibid*, Pl. X, 2.

[2] *Ibid*, Pl. X, 9—10.

[3] *Ibid*, Pl. X, 9—10.

[4] *Ibid*, Pl. X, 4—7

[5] Annual Rep. Arch. Survey of India, 1908—09, p. 247.

No inscription, which can safely be assigned to the 1st century B. C. or A. D., has been found anywhere in North-Eastern India, except at Sārnāth. The records which can be assigned to the 1st century B. C. are very few in number:

(*i*) Inscription on the upper side of the lower horizontal bar of the stone-railing surrounding the old stūpa in the south chapel of the main shrine [1]. The second half of the inscription only, is of earlier date, the first half belonging to the second century A. D. (not the 3rd or 4th as Messrs. Konow and Marshall imagine). The date of the second half also has not been correctly given. It is impossible to assign it to the 2nd century B. C. The shortening of the verticals in *pa* and *ha*, as well as the curvature in the base line of *na*, indicates that the record must be assigned to the 1st century B. C.

(*ii*) "When clearing the south chapel, the top of a stone railing became visible above the floor * * * a short votive inscription on one of the stones, places the erection of the railing in or before the 1st century B.C."[2] Here also the second part of the inscription only can be referred to the first century B.C. This part consists of the word "*Parigahetāvaṁ*".

(*iii*) Inscriptions on the pillars of a railing around a votive stūpa.[3] The first of these inscriptions (No. III) probably belongs to the 2nd century B.C. The probable reading is :—*Sihāye Sāhijāteyikāye thabho.* The second inscription (No. IV) has been very badly preserved. The fac-simile shows :—

1. ...*niya Sonade* (*va*).

---

[1] Annual Report of the Archæological Survey of India, 1906—07, p. 96, No. IV.

[2] *Ibid*, 1904-5, p. 68, Pl. XXXII, No. IX.

[3] *Ibid*, Pl. XXXII, Nos. III and IV, p. 102.

2. *Thabho dāna (ṁ).*

"The pillar-gift of Sonadeva (*Svarṇadeva*) of........." Inscription No. II which ends with the word "*Dānaṁ thabho* undoubtedly belongs to the early Maurya period of the 3rd century B. C.

(*iv*) Inscription on a rail stone (? cross bar) :—
Bhariniye Sahaṁ Yateyikā (ye)[1]—the gift of Yateyikā with Bharini. This inscription also belongs to the 1st century B.C., as indicated by the form of medial *i* and the shortening of the verticals in *ya*.

(*v*) Inscription of the king Aśvaghoṣa, the year 40. incised on the pillar of Aśoka.............." "............. *rparigeyhe rājña Aśvaghoshasya chatariśe Savachhare hematapakhe prathame divase dasame*."[2] Certain words following the above record, have been read by Dr. Venis as follows : *Sutithage 4, 200, 9.*[3] Drs. Fleet and Venis hold that this date should be referred to the *Mālava-Vikrama* era and arrive at 111-151 A.D. as the date of Aśvaghoṣa. If Drs. Fleet and Venis be correct, then it shall have to be admitted that, *Kaṇiṣka, Huviṣka* and *Vāsudeva* reigned in the latter half of the second and third centuries A.D., because in a treatise on Palaeography, it is impossible to admit, that the group of Kuṣāṇa inscriptions, came before those of *Aśvaghoṣa*, the *Kṣatrapas Nahapāna* and *Śoḍāsa*, and the archaic inscriptions from Mathurā.

(*vi*) Fragmentary inscriptions of the time of Aśvagho a :—

1. *Rājña Aśvaghoṣa (sya)*.........

---

[1] *Ibid*, 1906-7, p. 95, No. II, Pl. XXX.
[2] Ep. Ind. Vol., VIII, p. 171.
[3] J. R. A. S., 1912, pp. 701-707.

2. *Upala he ma (ṁtapakhe ?)*[1] ....

The principal characteristics of the above inscriptions from Sārnāth are :—

(*i*) total absence of any difference from the forms of the characters of the 1st and 2nd centuries B. C. found in North-Western India ;

(*ii*) consequently we find the general shortening of vertical lines, angularisation of curved strokes, and in the case of mẹdial vowel signs, cursiveness of the angular forms of the older Maurya Brāhmī.

D. Kuṣāna Inscriptions.

Under the above title the inscriptions of the great Kuṣāṇa Kings, Kaṇiṣka, Huviṣka and Vāsudeva are to be considered, the dates in whose inscriptions are generally taken to be Śaka dates.[2] At present two theories are current about the dates used in the inscriptions of the Kuṣāna kings mentioned above.

(*i*) That the dates in the Ku aṇa incriptions should be referred to the Mālava-Vikrama era which was established by Kaṇiṣka in the year 57 B. C. The expounders of this theory hold that the inscriptions of the Satraps Śoḍāsa and Rañjuvula fall after those of Kaṇiṣka, Huviṣka and Vāsudeva in the chronological order. This fact cannot, for a moment, be considered to be true, in a paper on Palæography.

(*ii*) That the dates in the Kuṣāṇa inscriptions should be referred to the Śaka era, which was founded by Kaṇiṣka in the year 78 A.D. In the following pages I have adopted this theory, which was started by Oldenberg

---

[1] Ep. Ind., Vol.. VIII., p. 172.

[2] Bühler's Indian Palæography (Eng. Ed.), p. 40 and Ind. Ant., Vol. XXXVII, p. 25.

and Fergusson, adopted by Bühler and Rapson, defended by myself and finally accepted by Mr. V. A. Smith. The inscriptions of the Ku āṇa period (1st and 2nd centuries A.D.) are more abundant in North-Western India. On this point Bühler says: "The next step in the development of Brāhmī of Northern India is illustrated by the inscriptions from the time of the Kuṣāṇa kings Kaniṣka, Huviṣka and Vāsuṣka-Vāsudeva, the first among whom made an end of the rule of the older Sakas in the Eastern and Southern Punjab. The inscriptions with the names of these kings which run from the years 4 to 98 (according to the usually accepted opinions, of the Saka era of A.D. 77-78, or of the 4th century of the Selukid era) are very numerous in Mathurā and its neighbourhood, and are found also in Eastern Rājputāna and in the Central India Agency (Sāñci)." [1]

In subsequent years a number of inscriptions have been discovered in North-Eastern India, which can without doubt be referred to this particular period :—

(*i*) the Bodh-Gayā Fragmentary inscription on the diamond throne (*vajrāsana*) ;[2]

(*ii*) the Sārnāth Umbrella-staff inscription of the 3rd year of Kāṇiṣka ;[3]

(*iii*) the inscription on the base of the Bodhisattva Image dedicated in the 3rd year of Kaṇiṣka ;[4]

(*iv*) the inscription at the back of the Bodhisattva image of the 3rd year of Kāṇiṣka ;[5]

---

[1] *Ibid.*

[2] Cunningham's Mahābodhi, p. 58.

[3] Epi. Ind., Vol. VIII, p. 176.

[4] *Ibid*, p. 179.

[5] *Ibid.*

(*v*) inscription on the pedestal of an image of Bodhisattva from Sāhet Māhet (the ancient Śrāvastī);[1]

(*vi*) inscription on an umbrella-staff, now in the Indian Museum, probably found in the ruins of Sāhet Māhet;[2]

(*vii*) inscription on the pedestal of an image of Bodhisattva found at Sāhet Māhet;[3]

(*viii*) fragmentary inscription on a fragment of a sculpture discovered at Rājagṛha (*Rājgir*), in the Pātnā District;[4]

(*ix*) fragmentary inscription on the pedestal of an image discovered at Rājagṛha;[5]

The records of the 1st century A.D. fall into two distinct and separate classes.—

I. *The Eastern variety of the North-Indian Alphabet of the Kusāṇa period, earlier variety.* All the inscriptions enumerated above belong to this class. Six years ago, I stated, that inscription No. VIII belongs to the class of Epigraphs known as inscriptions written in the Northern-Kṣatrapa alphabet, but now I agree with Dr. Vogel in calling them by the new name "*Early Kuṣāṇa.*" Inscription No. I. is by far the oldest inscription of the Kuṣāṇa period, discovered up to date, in North-Eastern India. It was incised on the edge of a slab of stone, which is at present lying under the Bodhi tree, at Bodh-Gayā.[6] It was in a very bad state of preservation

---

[1] Arch. Survey, Rep., Vol. I, p. 339 f.; J R.A.S., N.S., Vol. V, p. 192 J. A. S. B., 1898, p. 274 and Ep. Ind., Vol. VIII, p. 179.

[2] Epi. Ind., Vol. IX, p. 290.

[3] Annual Rep. Arch. Survey of India, 1908-9, p. 133.

[4] Ind., Ant., Vol. XXXVIII, p. 49.

[5] Annual Rep. Arch. Survey of India, 1905-6, pp. 105-6.

[6] Cunningham's Mahābodhi, Pl. X, ii; XIII and XIV.

PLATE III.

Inscription of the time of Mahendrapala-Ramgaya-Gaya.

at that time and has since suffered much from the weather. When I examined the stone in 1906, I found that the fragmentary inscription, was almost illegible. The use of the broad-backed *śa*, the shortening of the verticals in *pa*, and the *ma* in which the lower part is invariably triangular in form, show that the inscription belongs to the early Ku āṇa period. Yet, the doubtful *ya* in the opposite corner of the inscription, which is archaic in form, proved that the record must be referred to a period slightly earlier than those, in which the later, fully developed tripartite form of *ya* is found to be used.

II. *The Eastern variety of the North-Indian Alphabet of the Kuṣāṇa period, later variety.* No inscription, which can be safely referred to this class, has been discovered as yet in any part of North-Eastern India.

The principal characteristics of the earlier variety of the North-Eastern Kuṣāṇa alphabets are :—

(*i*) the use of the broad-backed *śa* :—*daṇḍaśca* and *Śāvastiye* (L. 2 Srāvastī image-inscription, Indian Museum), *daṇḍaśca* (L. 7), *Śāvastiye* (L. 8) of the Indian Museum umbrella-staff inscription, *Śivadhar-asya*, *Śrāvāsta* (L. 1), *kuśalā*, *bhuyakuśalaṁ*, and *Śiva-mitrena* (L. 3) of the new Bodhisattva image-inscription from Sāhet Māhet, *Śakyamuni*, on the fragmentary sculpture from Rājgir; *Indraśiri* and *Parahaśalika* (L. 2) in the inscription on the newly discovered pedestal from Rājgir;

(*ii*) the lingual *ṣa*, angular in form in which the cross-bar does not reach the left vertical line: *Kaniṣkasya* (L. 1), *bhikṣusya*, *Puṣya* (L. 2), *yaṣṭi* and *pratiṣṭhāpito* (L. 4), *kṣatrapena* (L. 8), *pariṣā* (L. 9) of the Sārnāth Umbrella-staff inscription, *pratiṣṭhāpito* (L. 1), *kṣatra-pena*, *mahākṣatrapena* and *Vanaṣparena* in (L. 2) of the inscription on the pedestal of the Sārnāth Bodhisattva image; *Kaniṣka* (L. 1), *bhikṣusya* (L. 2), *yaṣṭi* (L. 3) of the inscription on the back of the Bodhisattva image from Sārnāth; *bhikṣusya* and *Puṣya* (L. 1) *bhikṣusya* (L. 2) in the inscription on the pedestal of the Bodhisattva image in the Indian Museum found at Sāhet Māhet; *kṣatriyānaṁ, veliṣṭānaṁ* (L. 1): *vīcakṣaṇa* (L. 2) on the inscription on the pedestal of the new image from Sāhet Māhet. It should be noted in this connection, that the form of the subscript lingual *ṣa,* as found in *kṣatriyānaṁ* (L. 1) and *vīçakṣaṇa* (L. 2), is still more archaic, having the cursive form of the older Maurya alphabet;

(*iii*) the cursive form of *ha,* which seems to have been derived from the cursive forms of the Jaugaḍa separate edicts and the Kausambı edict on the Allahabad pillar: this form occurs on one inscription only, *viz.* on the pedestal of the new Bodhisattva image from Sāhet Māhet; *Bohisatva* (L. 1—3),[1] but in all other cases the angular form of *ha* is found to have been used;

(*iv*) in the majority of cases, the subscript *ya* has the tripartite form. The only exceptions being *Puṣya* in (L. 1) of the inscription on the pedestal of the Bodhisattva image from Śrāvastī, now in the Indian Museum and in *Śakyamuni* on the fragmentary sculpture from Rājgir, which is also in the Indian Museum. The dearth of inscriptions, written in characters of the later variety of the Northern Kuṣaṇa alphabet, in Eastern India has already been noticed above. Inscriptions of the 3rd and 4th centuries A.D., are also very rare in the whole of the Northern India. With the exception of two inscriptions from Mathurā, which I hold to belong to the 3rd century

[1] Annual Rep. Arch. Survey of India, 1908-09, p. 135.

A.D.[1] and which others hold to belong to the 6th century A.D.[2], no inscriptions are known which can be said to belong to the pre-Gupta period.

At the beginning of the Gupta period, we are confronted with three distinct varieties of the alphabet, used in Northern India. Inscriptions belonging to the first-half of the 4th century A.D., are unknown unless the Allahabad pillar-inscription of Samudragupta[3] be referred to that period. The second inscription in the chronological order, which can be safely referred to this period, is the Bodh-Gayā Image-inscription[4] of the Gupta year 64=383-84 A.D. Scholars are divided in opinion about the date of this inscription also. Prof. Lüders of Berlin holds Cunningham's theory and says that it is a *Śaka* date[5], inspite of Dr. Bühler's clear statement on the point.[6]

E. The so-called Gupta Alphabet of the 4th and 5th centuries A.D.

Dr. Bühler recognises three different varieties in the Northern Indian alphabet of the 4th and 5th centuries A. D. :—

(*i*) the Eastern variety—distinguished by the peculiar forms of *la*, *ha*, *ṣa* and *sa*,[7]

(*ii*) the Western variety—cursive roundhand type,[8]

---

[1] Ind. Ant., Vol. XXXVII, p. 29.

[2] Fleet's Gupta Inscriptions, pp. 262, 273; Kielhorn's List of Inscriptions of Northern India, Ep. Ind., Vol. V, App. p. 63, No. 445 and p. 65, No. 463.

[3] Fleet's Gupta Inscriptions, p. 1.

[4] Cunningham's Mahābodhi, Pl. XXV.

[5] Ind. Ant., Vol. XXXIII, p. 40.

[6] Bühler's Indian Palæography, Eng. Ed., p. 46 and note 10

[7] *Ibid*, Eng. Ed., p. 46.

[8] *Ibid*, p. 47.

and (*iii*) the Western variety—angular monumental type.[1]

In the light of later discoveries, especially the important finds of the British and Prussian expeditions into Central Asia under Sir Marc Aurel Stein, Grünwedel and others, the Northern Indian alphabet of the 4th and 5th centuries A. D., should be divided into the following varieties :—

1. The Eastern variety : specimens —
   (*i*) the Allahabad pillar-inscription of Samudragupta,
   (*ii*) the Udayagiri cave-inscription of Candragupta II,
   (*iii*) the Gaḍhwā fragmentary inscriptions of the times of Candragupta II and Kumāragupta I,
   (*iv*) the Dhānāidaha grant of Kumāragupta I,
   (*v*) the Mānkuwār inscription of Kumāragupta I,
   (*vi*) the Bihār pillar-inscription of Skandagupta,
   (*vii*) the Kosām image-inscription of Bhīmavarman,
   (*viii*) the Kahāuṁ pillar-inscription of Skandagupta.
2. The Western variety : specimens —
   (*i*) the Mathurā inscription of Candragupta II,
   (*ii*) the Sāñcī inscription of Candragupta II,
   (*iii*) the Bharadi Ḍih or Karamdanda inscription of Kumāragupta I,
   (*iv*) the Bhiṭāri pillar-inscription of Skandagupta,
   (*v*) the Indore grant of Skandagupta,
   (*vi*) the Erān pillar-inscription of Budhagupta.

---

[1] *Ibid.*

3. The Southern variety: specimens —

(*i*) the Bilsaḍ pillar-inscription of Kumāragupta I,

(*ii*) the Gangdhar inscription of Viśvavarman,

(*iii*) the Mandaśor inscription of Kumāragupta I, and Bandhuvarman,

(*iv*) the Vijayagaḍh inscription of the *Yaudheyas*

(*v*) the Vijayagaḍh pillar-inscription of Viṣṇuvardhana,

(*vi*) the Girnār (Junagaḍ) Rock inscription of Skandagupta.

4. The Central Asian variety: specimens —

(*i*) the Bower Manuscript,

(*ii*) numerous other manuscripts written in the Central Asiatic variety of the Gupta alphabet discovered by the British and German expeditions.

I. The Eastern Variety.

Twenty-one years ago, five years before the publication of Dr. Bühler's work on Indian Palæography, Dr. A. F. R. Hoernle recorded the following observations on the Indian script of the 4th and 5th centuries A. D.: "There existed at the time of the Gupta period two very distinct classes of the ancient Nāgarī alphabet, North Indian and the South Indian. The test letter for these two great classes is the character for *m*. The Northern class of alphabets, however, is again divided into two great sections which, though their areas overlapped to a certain extent, may be broadly, and for practical purposes sufficiently, distinguished as the Western and Eastern sections. The test letter in this case is the cerebral sibilant *sha* (*ṣa*)"[1] This classification was also adopted by the late Dr. Bühler, who added two more test letters: *la* and *ha*. "The differences between the Eastern and Western varieties of the so-called Gupta alphabet appear in the signs of *la*, *ṣa* and *ha*. In the Eastern variety, the left limb of *la* is turned sharply downwards: cf. the *la* of the Jaugaḍa separate edicts. Further the base stroke of *ṣa* is made round and attached as a loop to the slanting central bar. Finally the base stroke of *ha* is suppressed, and its hook, attached to the vertical, is turned sharply to the left, exactly as in the Jaggayyapeta inscriptions. In the Western variety these three letters have the older and fuller forms." Another test letter, of the Eastern alphabet of this period, is the dental sibilant *sa*. In the inscriptions of the Eastern variety, this letter always has a loop at the end of its left vertical line instead of the customary curve or hook, *cf.* the form of the letter in the Allahabad pillar-inscription of Samudragupta. This form of *sa* has also been found in the inscriptions of the Kuṣāṇa period, discovered in Mathurā. The Kaṅkālīṭīlā inscription of the 25th year, shows that, in that inscription, all cases of *sa*, have this form.[2]

The characteristics of the epigraphic alphabet of the 4th and 5th centuries A.D. have already been discussed at length by Dr Bühler.[3] It will only be necessary to trace the history of the development of the Eastern variety in the following pages. In 1891, Dr. Hoernle perceived that, "in India proper, the North-eastern alphabet gradually came to be entirely displaced by the North-western alphabet, in comparatively very early times. This

---

[1] J. A. S. B., 1891, Pt. I., p. 81.

[2] Epi. Ind., Vol. I, p. 384, No. v.

[3] Bühler's Indian Palæography, Eng. Ed., p. 47.

displacement must have been in progress during the earlier part of the sixth century A.D. and must have been completed about 580 A.D., for in 588 A.D., we already find inscriptions in Bodh-Gayā (inscription of Mahānāman, Fleet, p. 274), which show an exclusive North-Western character. There is not a single inscription known, so far as I am aware, about and after 600 A.D., which show the distinctive marks of the old North-Eastern alphabet."[1] This statement will have to be examined in the light of later discoveries made during the last two decades—

(*i*) The Dhānāidaha grant of Kumāragupta I, G.E. 113 = 432 A.D.[2]

(*ii*) The Mathurā Jaina image-inscription of the time of Kumāragupta I, G.E. 113 = 432 A.D.[3]

(*iii*) The Karamdaṇḍa image-inscription of Kumāragupta I, G.E. 117 = 436 A.D.[4]

(*iv*) The Amaunā plate of the Mahārāja Nandana, G.E. 232 = 531 A.D.[5]

(*v*) The Paṭiakellā grant of the Mahārāja Śivarāja; G.E. 283 = 602 A.D.[6]

(*vi*) The Gañjām grant of the time of Mahārājādhirāja Śaśāṅka, G.E. 300 = 619 A.D.[7]

(*vii*) The Muṇḍeśvarī inscription of Mahāsāmanta Mahāprātīhāra Mahārāja Udayasena, the Har a year 30 = 636 A.D.[8]

---

[1] J. A. S. B., 1891, Pt. I, p 82.

[2] J. A. S. B. (N.S.), Vol. V, p. 459.

[3] Epi. Ind., Vol. II, p. 210, No. XXXIX.

[4] J. A. S. B. (N.S.), Vol. V, p. 457; and Ep. Ind., Vol. X, p. 70.

[5] *Ibid*, p. 49 and J. A. S. B. Vol. V, N. S. p. 164.

[6] Epi. Ind., Vol. IX, p. 285.

[7] Epi. Ind., Vol. VI, p. 141.

[8] *Ibid*, Vol. IX, p. 289.

(*viii*) The Purī grant of Sainyabhīta-Mādhavarāja II.[1]

(*ix*) The Parikuḍ grant of Madhyamarāja, the Harṣa year 88=694 A.D.[2]

The Eastern variety of the epigraphic Alphabet of Northern India of the 4th and 5th centuries A.D. did merge, as Dr. Hoernle has observed, into the Western variety. Inscriptions, discovered after the publication of Dr. Hoernle's article, show the gradual changes in the epigraphic alphabet of the 5th and 6th centuries A.D., and tend to prove that this change is already in evidence in the first half of the 5th century. This displacement of the Eastern variety of the alphabet of this period by the Western must have been completed before the end of the first half of the 6th century.

The Allahabad pillar-inscription of Samudragupta shows the fully developed form of the Eastern variety and the test letters can be observed here to their best advantage. The next inscription, in the chronological order, in which the Eastern alphabet has been used, is the Udayagiri cave-inscription of Candragupta II, on which Dr. Bühler observes "The fact that Fleet's No. 6 is found far west, near Bhilsā in Mālva, may be explained by its having been incised during an expedition of Candragupta II, to Mālva, at the command of his minister, who calls himself an inhabitant of Pāṭaliputra."[3] Next we come to two new inscriptions both of which were incised in the year 113 of the Gupta era=432 A.D.—

(*i*) The Mathurā Jaina image-inscription.

(*ii*) The Dhānāidaha grant.

---

[1] J. A. S. B., 1904, Pt. I, p. 284, Pl. VI.

[2] Baṅgīya-Sāhitya-Pariṣad-Patrikā, Vol. XVI, p. 185, also Epi. Ind., Vol. XI, p. 281.

[3] Bühler's Indian Palæography, Eng. Ed., p. 46.

PLATE IV.

Dinajpur pillar inscription—Saka 888 (?).

As both of these records mention Kumāragupta I by name, so there cannot be any doubt as to their proper date. The Mathurā inscription shows the typical forms of the Western variety.[1] In the Dhānāidaha grant of Kumāragupta I, we find—

(*i*) in all cases, the looped form of the dental sibilant *śa*, has been used,

(*ii*) in all cases, the looped form of the lingual sibilant *ṣa*, has been used,

(*iii*) in all cases, the hooked form of *ha*, has been used,

(*iv*) in the majority of cases the hooked form of *la* has been used. In one solitary instance the Western variety form has succeeded in replacing the older one, *viz* :—*Vakkralaṇa* (?) in L. 8.[2]

But in a stone-inscription incised sixteen years later, we find Eastern variety forms of *sa*, *ṣa* and *ha* in all cases. In the Mānkuwār inscription of Kumāragupta I, we see that *ṣa*, *sa* and *ha* have not changed in the year 129 G. E.=448 A.D. The discrepancy may be explained thus. The current script of a country, as found on copper-plates, generally shows a more advanced form than that of the Epigraphic alphabet, found in stone-inscriptions. Copper-plates, in ancient India, should be taken to belong to the same class of records, as paper manuscripts or papyri of other countries. The forms of the alphabet used in them should be distinguished from the forms used in epigraphs proper. Twelve years later than the date of this inscription, we find the Eastern forms of *ṣa*, *sa*, *la* and *ha* still persisting in all cases, in the Kahāuṁ pillar-inscription of Skandagupta, of

[1] Epi. Ind., Vol. II, p. 210, No. XXXIX.

[2] J. A. S. B. (N. S.), Vol. Pl. XX, p. 461.

G.E. 141 = 460 A.D. But in an undated inscription of the same king, we see that the Western forms are gradually taking the place of Eastern ones. In the Bihār pillar-inscription of Skandagupta, the first half of the record shows uses of Eastern forms in the majority of cases :—

I. *la*—(*i*) *tulya*, (*ii*) *atulyaḥ* (L 1), (*iii*) *atulya* (L. 3), (*iv*) *maṇḍalaṁ* (L. 5), (*v*) *vyālamba* (L. 7), (*vi*) *lokān* (L. 9), (*vii*) *kāla* (L. 11)

II. *ha*—(*i*) *hi havya* (L. 4), (*ii*) *gṛhaṁ* (L. 8);

Only in one instance we find a Western variety form, *viz* :—*agrahāre* (L. 13). But in the second half of the record, we find that the Western variety form of *ha* has invariably been used, in all cases. In the second half of this record there are two instances of *la* :—(*i*) *kulaḥ* (L. 28) and *saulkika* (L. 29) but as the facsimile given in Dr. Fleet's work is incomplete and does not contain these lines, it is not possible to compare the forms of *la* used in the second half of the inscription with those of the first half. I have found that the Bihār pillar-inscription has suffered much from exposure in the weather, after the publication of Dr. Fleet's work, and at present it is not possible to get a clearer, and more complete, inked impression than the one taken for Dr. Fleet. On the clear evidence of the Bihār inscription of Skandagupta, we have the fact that Western forms were replacing the Eastern ones in the alphabet of North-Eastern India in the first half of the 5th century A.D. The Pāli grant of Lakṣmaṇa, of the Gupta year 158[1] = 477 A.D., shows no form, in the alphabet used, which has any resemblance to those of the Eastern variety. The Pāli grant should be included among North-Eastern inscriptions, instead of North-Western ones, as it was found about thirty miles from Allahabad

[1] Epi. Ind., Vol. II, p. 363.

It may be mentioned that the Kosām image- inscription of Bhīmavarman, of the Gupta year 139=458 A.D., shows the use of eastern forms and the findspot of this record is close to Pāli. In this inscription, we find that, all the test letters, *ṣa*, *sa*, *ha* and *la*, have assumed Western forms. The evidence of the Pāli grant of Lakṣmaṇa is further borne out by the alphabet used in the Amaunā grant of Nandana, of the Gupta year 232[1]=551 A.D. This inscription was discovered in the Gayā District of Bihar and Orissa and cannot be referred to any other class of inscription but the North-Eastern. In this inscription we find that *ṣa*, *sa*, *ha* and *la* are of the western variety. Consequently we are now in a position to reconsider the statement made by Dr. Hoernle twenty-one years ago: "This displacement must have been in progress during the earlier part of the 6th century A.D., and must have been completed about 580 A.D., for in 588 A.D., we already find inscriptions in Bodh-Gayā (Inscription of Mahānāman, Fleet, p. 274) which show an exclusive North-Western character."[2] We are now in a position to state definitely that the movement towards the adoption of Western variety forms in North-Eastern inscriptions was already in evidence in the 4th decade of the 5th century A.D. So early as the days of the Gupta emperor Skandagupta, the change had already affected the epigraphic alphabet of the time. The displacement was completed before the eighth decade of the 5th century and all traces of Eastern variety forms or characters had disappeared from the plains of Northern India, before the beginning of the 6th century A.D.

---

[1] *Ibid*, Vol. X, p. 49.

[2] J. A. S. B., 1891, pt. I, p. 82.

We should now proceed to the Palæographical examination of a class of records, about which there is much difference of opinion. I refer to the four copper-plate inscriptions, which have been discovered at various times during the last three decades. The first three was published by Mr. F. E. Pargiter in 1910[1] and the last one was published by myself[2] as well as by Mr. Pargiter[3] in 1911. In size, script and composition the four records indicate that they belonged to the same variety. These four grants differ from all other copper-plate inscriptions discovered in India on the following points :—

(*i*) they are not grants of lands, made by any paramount sovereign, nor by any feudatory chief, with the sanction of his suzerain,

(*ii*) they purport to be deeds of transfer of property, made by certain local officials, to a private person, as well as deeds of grants, made by those private persons to certain Brāhmanas;

(*iii*) they mention a number of officials by their proper names, and not merely by designations, as usual.

The facts, quoted above, would alone go to prove that the records were spurious. But in addition to them, we have the palæographical evidence, which shows that the alphabets of two different periods and in the case of the last one, of three different periods, have been used in the composition of these inscriptions. In these records we find that, (1) *ṣa*, *la* and *ha* have two forms and often three; and are used in conjunction with forms of the sixth or even of the seventh or ninth centuries A.D. In the first grant: the grant of Dharmāditya of the year 3, we find

---

[1] Ind. Ant., Vol. XXXIX, p. 193.

[2] J. A. S. B., Vol. VI, p. 435.

Ibid, Vol. VII, p. 476.

that two different forms have been used, in the case of three test letters *ṣa*, *la* and *ha*.

I. *Ṣa* :—

(*i*) *Eastern variety.*

1. *Ambarīṣa* (L. 1), 2. *viṣayapati* (L. 3), 3. *viṣaya-mahattara* (L. 4), 4. *Ghoṣacandra* (L. 5), 5. *kṣettra* (L. 7), 6. *viṣaye* (L. 8), 7. *viṣaye* (L. 10), 8-9. *kṣettrāṇi* and *kṣettra* (L. 11), 10. *dṛṣṭi* (L. 12), 11. *ṣaḍ-bhāgaḥ* (L. 13), 12. *abhilāṣa* (L. 14), 13. *ṣalaṅga*, (L. 19), 14. *modaneṣu* (L. 21).

(*ii*) *Western variety.* Strictly speaking, the forms of the letter, used in the following words, are much later in date than the North-Western Gupta alphabet. In all cases, the letter is found in the ligature *kṣa* and we find that peculiar curvature before *ka* denoting the presence of the *ṣa*, which we see for the first time in the inscriptions of Ādityasena and those of the Gāhaḍavāla princes of Kanauj[1], in the 11th and 12th centuries A. D. There are five instances of this later form in the first grant—

1. *kṣettra* (L. 16), 2. *anugrahākāṁkṣiṇā* (L. 18), 3. *kṣepa* (L. 21), 4. *dakṣiṇeṇa* (L. 23), 5. *kṣeṇī*. (L. 25).

II. *La* :—

(*i*) *Eastern variety.*

1. *lavdha* (L. 2), 2. *kālasakha* (L. 5-6), 3. *durllabha* (*L.* 6), 4. *lābhaḥ* (L. 13), 5. *saṁkalpābhiḥ* (L. 14), 6. *Śīlakuṇḍaś=ca* (L. 214).

(*ii*) *Western Variety.*

1. *kāle* and 2. *vārakamaṇḍale* (L. 3), 3. *āluka* (L. 5), 4. *kuṇḍalipta* and 5. *kulasvāmi* (L. 6) 6.

---

[1] Bühler's Indian Palæography, pl. IV, XVIII, 45 & pl. V, XII, XX, 44.

mūlyaṁ (L. 8), 7. *pustapāla* (L. 9), 8. *kulya* and *khaṇḍala* (L. 11), 10. *kalanā* (L. 12), 11. *abhilāṣa* (L. 14), 12. *nalena* (L. 16), 13. *dhruvilāṭyāṁ* (L. 16), 14. *kulya* (L. 16), 15. *kāla* (L. 18), 16. *ṣal-aṅga* (L. 19), 17. *uparilikhita* (L 20), 18. *anupālana* (L.21), 19. *pratipālanīyaṁ* (L. 22), 20. *liṅgāni* (L. 23).

III. Ha :—

(*i*) *Eastern variety.*

1. *vṛhac-caṭṭa* (L. 4), 2. *icchāmy-ahaṁ* (L. 7), 3. *brāhmaṇasya*, 4. *gṛhītvā* (L. 8), 5. *avadhṛtam=astī=ha* (L. 10), 6. *hastena* (L. 15), 7. *paratr=ānugraha* (L. 18), 8. *himasena* (L. 23).

(*ii*) *Western variety,*

1. *mahārājādhirāja* and 2. *mahārāja* (L. 2), 3. *mahattara* (L. 4), 4. *tad-arhatha* (L. 8), 5. *mātā-pitror-anugraha* (L. 19), 6. *haret* (L. 26), 7. *himase·a* (L. 25), 8. *saha* (L. 26).

Similarly in the second grant from Faridpur we find that—

I. In all cases the Western variety form of *ha* has been used.

II. The Eastern variety form of *la* has been used in one case only *e.g.* in *maṇḍala* (L. 4). In all other we find the Western variety forms—

1. *lavdha* (L. 3), 2. *kāle* (L. 4), 3. *gopāla* (L.5), 4. *khaṇḍalakaiḥ* (L. 9), 5. *lauhitya* (L. 11), 6. *kulya* (L. 14), 7. *akhila* (L. 15), 8. *satpālāni* (L. 17), 9. *khaṇḍalaka* (L. 17), 10. *pustapāla* (L. 18), 11. *dharmmaśīla* and 12. *nalena* (L. 19), 13. *liṅgāni* (L. 20), 14. *ślokāni* (L. 24).

The form in the last example is very late. It is the 9th century form, found for the first time in the Dighwā-Dubhauli grant of Mahendrapāla[1].

III. In the case of the lingual *ṣa* we find eastern variety forms in :

1. *Nahuṣa* (L. 1), 2. *Ambarīṣa* (L. 2), 3. *viṣaya* (L. 5), 4. *Jyeṣra* (L. 7), 5. *Somaghoṣa* and 6. *viṣayānāṁ* (L. 8) 7. *ṣaṣṭha* (L. 16) 8. *vṛkṣa* (L. 21), 9. *ṣaṣṭiṁ* and 10. *Varṣa* (L. 24), 11. *śva-viṣṭhāyāṁ* (L. 27) and western variety ones in :

1. *kṣettra* (L. 9), 2. *kṣet rāṇi* (L. 14), 3. *ākṣeptā* (L 25); another indistinct form is to be found in *hast-āsṭaka.* The late seventh or eleventh century form of *kṣa* is found in *kṣettra* in L. 17.

The third plate is in a very bad state of preservation and the facsmile published with Mr. Pargiter's article is very indistinct ; the reverse or the second side of the plate only, is capable of being analysed for palaeographical purposes. In it, we find, that in all recognisable cases, the lingual *ṣa* is of the Eastern variety of the early Gupta alphabet. Both forms of *ha* have been used. Only one instance of the Western variety is legible :—*maha* in L. 3. In all other instances where the record is legible we find the use of the Eastern variety :—(1) *mahattaraḥ* (L. 8-9), (2) *hastāṣṭaka* (L. 10), (3) *agrahāra* (L. 22), (4) *har-ta* (L. 24), (5) *saha* (L. 25).

So also in the case of *la* we find that the Eastern variety form has been rarely used while the Western variety form is common :—

I. Eastern variety :—(*i*) *Vatsapāla* (L. 5), (*ii*) *'ıṅgāni* (L. 21).

---

[1] Ind. Ant., Vol. XV, p. 112.

II. Western variety:—(*i*) *mūlyam* (L. 14), (*ii*) *kulavārān* (L. 18), (*iii*) *prakalpya* (L. 18), (*iv*) *dharmaśīla* (L. 19), (*v*) *nalena* (L. 19), (*vi*) *Vatsapāla* (L. 19), (*vii*) *kulya* (L. 20), (*viii*) *Dhruvilāṭa* (L. 22), (*ix*) *Śīlakuṇḍa* (L. 23).

It should be noted in this connection that in the majority of cases we find the bipartite form of *ya*. In the fourth grant we find, that in all cases the bipartite form of *ya*, the Western variety form of the lingual *ṣa* and *la* have been used. With the exception of three instances, *ha* also has the Western variety form. These three instances are:—(1) *vrahmaṇ-opāya* (L. 11), (2) *vrāhmaṇa* (L. 14), (3) *sahasrāṇi* (L. 20-21). In addition to these, we find later forms, in the word *parkkaṭṭi* (L. 18) and *svāminah* (L. 17). in case of *ka* and *na* respectively. In conclusion, we may freely say, that all four copper plates are forged. It may be asserted that, the plates belong to the transitional period, when Eastern variety forms were gradually being displaced by Western ones. But, the use of mediaeval forms, precludes such a possibility:—(1) I have already commented on the form of the ligature *ksa* in the first plate. (2) Another, much later form, is that of *śa*, in the date of the first plate, which occurs for the first time in the Aphsaḍ inscription of Adityasena and Dighwā-Dubhauli grant of Mahendrapāla, the Pratīhara, of V. E. 955=898 A.D. The form of *ka* in *parkkaṭṭi* and *na* in *svaminaḥ* in the fourth grant had already been commented upon. Consequently we find that the four copper-plate inscriptions, being forgeries, are of no use in a palaeographical discussion.

PLATE V.

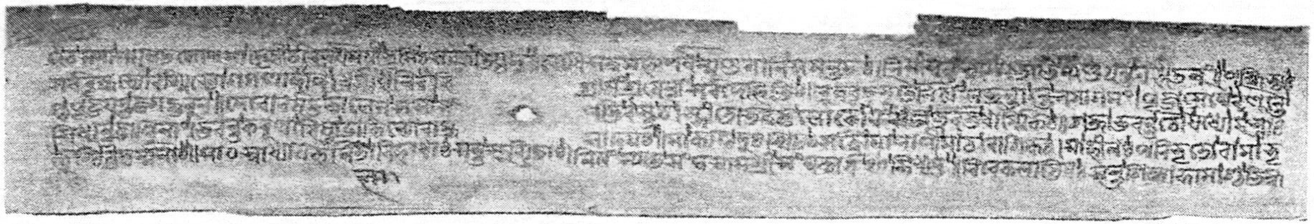

Bodhicaryavatara (Ms. Ga 8067) Fol. 65, obv. A. S. B.

CHAPTER III

The Eastern Alphabet—550-1100 A.D.

We now come to the class of alphabets, to which Dr. Bühler has given the name, *Siddhamātrkā*. From this point, Dr. Bühler's work ceases to be exhaustive and does not deal with Eastern variety forms of the Northern alphabet, separately. Such a treatment of North-Indian palaeography was, perhaps, impossible sixteen years ago, and consequently, the author of the *Indian Palæography* was obliged to deal with the Northern Indian alphabet of the 6th, 7th, 8th, 9th and 10th centuries A.D., as a single whole. The differentiation was made only in the case of Śāradā alphabet, which was already a separate unit in the 8th century A.D. and in a much later period, in the case of proto-Bengali. In these pages Dr. Bühler's arrangement has not been followed, on account of the following reasons :—

I. The discovery of a number of dated records, has made it impossible to accept, the alphabet used in the Bodh-Gayā inscription of Mahānāman, as representing type specimens of the North-Eastern alphabet of the 6th and 7th centuries A.D. These new inscriptions are :—

(*i*) the Amaunā grant of Nandana[1], G. E. 232=551 A.D.

(*ii*) the Paṭiakellā grant of Mahārāja Śivarāja[2], G. E. 283=602 A.D.

(*iii*) the Gañjām grant of the time of Mahārājādhirāja Śaśāṅka[3], G. E. 300=619 A.D.

---

[1] Epi. Ind., Vol. X, p. 49.

[2] *Ibid*, Vol. IX. p. 285.

[3] *Ibid*, Vol. VI. p. 142.

(*iv*) The Muṇḍeśvarī inscription of the Mahāsāmanta Mahāpratīhāra Mahārāja Udayasena[1], H. E. 30=636 A. D.

II. The final settlement of the chronology of the Gurjjara-Pratīhāra dynasty of Northern and Central India, by the researches of Mr. D. R. Bhandarkar and the late Mr. A. M. T. Jackson, has placed the introduction of the Nāgarī alphabet into Northern India one hundred and thirt-yseven years later. On this point Dr. Bühler said "In Northern and Central India, the Nāgarī appears first on the copper-plate of the Mahārāja Vināyakapāla of Mahodaya probably of A. D. 794."[2] The real date of Vināyakapāla's grant is V. E. 988=931 A. D. instead of H. E. 188=794 A. D.[3]

III. The discovery of a number of inscriptions in North-Eastern India, specially of the Pāla kings of Bengal, makes it possible to distinguish two different varieties of the North-Eastern alphabet, as early as the 8th century A. D., and shows that Nāgarī has had very little influence on the development of the Bengali alphabet.

Sixteen years ago, the Bodh-Gayā inscription of Ma.ıānāman was the only known dated inscription of the 6th century A. D., in North-Eastern India. In it, Dr. Hoernle and Dr. Bühler, found, for the first time, that the Eastern variety of the early Gupta alphabet has been entirely d splaced by the Western one. But, we have already seen, that fresh discoveries place this displacement more than a century earlier. The next point to be considered is the tripartite form of *ya* and the downward limit of its use. In 1891 Dr. Hoernle fixed 600 A. D. as the

[1] *Ibid*, Vol. IX, p. 289.

[2] Bühler's Indian Palæography, Eng. Ed., p. 51.

[3] Epi. Ind., Vol. VIII, App. 1, pp. 1 & 4.

lowest limit for the use of this form of *ya* in Northern India :—

"Any inscription in the North-Western Indian alphabet, which shows the more or less exclusive use of the old form of *ya*, must date from before 600 A. D., while any inscription showing an exclusive use of the cursive form of *ya* must date after 600 A. D."[1]

The force of Dr. Hoernle's argument has been weakened by the discovery of the Udaypur inscription of the Guhila Aparājita[2], of V. E. 716=659 A.D. "The discovery of an inscription of the 7th century", observes Dr. Bühler, "with mostly tripartite *ya*, E. I. 4, 29, makes a modification of Hoernle's argument necessary but does not invalidate his final result".[3] It will be observed that no limit has been fixed for the use of the tripartite form of *ya* in a North-Eastern inscription. In the Bodh-Gayā inscription of Mahānāman, we find that, the bipartite form had, entirely, displaced the tripartite one. Consequently, it has been supposed that the bipartite form has displaced the tripartite form, in the North-Eastern inscriptions, almost about the same time as in North-western records. Subsequent discoveries now enable us to prove beyond doubt that in North-eastern India, the use of the tripartite form of *ya*, lasted about half a century longer than the limit of North-western India. For example we have the form used in the Amaunā grant of Nandana. The date of this inscription is not far removed from that of the Bodh-Gayā inscription, and it was found in a place not very far off from Bodh-Gayā, yet we find that in all cases the tripartite form of *ya* has been used. So again, in the case of Paṭiākellā grant of ivarāja, we find that

[1] J.A.S.B., 1891, pt. 1, p. 90.

[2] Epi. Ind., Vol. IV, p. 29.

[3] Bühler's Indian Palæography, p. 48. note 3.

the tripartite form is being used in all cases, in the Gupta year 283=602 A.D. So also in the case of the Muṇḍeśvarī inscription, we find that the tripartite form alone is used in 636 A. D. Consequently, we have to admit that the use of the bipartite form of *ya*, in the Bodh-Gayā inscription of Mahānāman, in the Gupta year 269=588 A.D., is premature. There are other reasons which lead us to believe that, though this record was found in North-Eastern India, the alphabet of the locality was not used in incising it, which on the other hand was done by a man from Western India. We have a similar case in the Bhitāri pillar-inscription of Skandagupta, which, though found in Eastern India, shows the use of the Western variety of the North-Indian alphabet; and the Sāñcī inscription of the time of Candragupta II which, though found in Western India shows the use of the Eastern variety of the alphabet. The alphabet used in the Bodh-Gayā inscription of Mahanaman cannot be taken to represent the ordinary Eastern variety of the Epigraphic alphabet of North-India in the 6th century A.D. for the following reasons :—

(1) the Amauna grant of Nandana and the Paṭiākella grant of Sivarāja show the exclusive use of the tripartite form of *ya*; consequently, we have to admit that in the Eastern variety of the Northern alphabet the tripartite form of *ya* was in use in the 6th century A.D. ;

(2) the prevalence of acute angles at the lower extremities of letters is exceptional, and, not of common occurrence, in these records.

The ordinary 6th century epigraphic alphabet of North-Eastern India is then to be found in the following inscriptions :—

(1) the Amaunā grant of Nandana,

(2) the Patiākellā grant of Śivarāja,

(3) the Barābār cave-inscription of Ananta-varman,[1]

(4) the Nāgārjunī cave-inscription of Ananta-varman,[2] and

(5) the Nāgārjunī cave-inscription of Ananta-varman.[3]

The principal characteristics of the alphabet, which remained current in North-eastern India, from 550-650 A.D. are noted below :

(1) The use of the tripartite form of *ya*. The only exception is the Ganjam grant of the time of Śaśāṅka. The difference cannot be accounted for at present, so long as the riddle of Śaśāṅka-Narendra remains unsolved. Why aśāṅka, probably surnamed Narendra, whose coinage is allied to that of the early or the Imperial Guptas, went to Kaliṅga and how he came to be acknôwledged as a suzerain, by the *Śailodbhava* princes of the *Koṅgoda-maṇḍala*,[4] is still a mystery to us. The introduction of the North-Eastern alphabet, into the Northern Sircars, was also probably due to this prince. We find the ordinary 6th century alphabet of Kaliṅga, in the Buguḍā grant of Madhavavarman [5] and the Parikuḍ plates of Madhyamarāja.[6]

(2) The general prevalence of right angles at the lower extremities of certain letters *e.g. gha, pa, pha, ṣa* and *sa*.

(3) The absence of later developments such as tails or verticals on the right of these signs.

---

[1] Fleet's Gupta Inscriptions, p. 221, pl. XXX B.

[2] *Ibid*, p. 224, pl. XXXI, A.

[3] *Ibid*, p. 227, pl. XXXI B.

[4] Epi. Ind., Vol. VI, p. 142.

[5] *Ibid*, Vol. III, p. 43 and Vol. VII, p. 100.

Vaṅgīya-Sāhitya-Pariṣad-Patrikā, Vol XVI, p. 197 ; Epi. Ind., Vol. XI, pp. 281-87.

In other words. the North-eastern epigraphic alphabet of the 6th century A.D., presents the ordinary characteristics of the North-western variety of the early Gupta alphabet.

Early in the latter-half of the 7th century A.D., we find a marked change in the North-Eastern alphabet. The Shahpur image-inscription of the Harsa year 66=671 A.D. and the undated Aphsaḍ inscription, both of the time of Ādityasena of Magadha, exhibit this change for the first time. From this time onward, the eastern variety of the northern alphabet, develops by itself and the western variety never succeeds in displacing it again. For a short time only, during the domination of the Gurjjara-Pratīhāra princes, a western variety, called Nāgarī, makes its influence felt and divides the eastern variety into two different branches. Out of these sub-divisions, the western one is gradually absorbed in Nāgarī, while the eastern one develops separately and becomes the Bengali script, of the 11th and 12th centuries A.D. At this period, it is necessary to take a more complete survey of the Eastern alphabet, than that done in the case of the Eastern variety of previous centuries. In the latter half of the 7th century A. D., we find the following characteristics of the eastern variety of the northern alphabet.—

I. Vowels.

(1) The upper part of the left limb of *a* has become a slightly elongated nail-head or wedge, while the lower part is converted into a regular curve, with a knob at its top, looking more like a comma. The right limb together with the line joining both the limbs, can be drawn at one stroke of the pen and the letter resembles the Bengali one, in its present form. Cf. *a* in *ajanayad* (in L. 6).

(2) In the case of *ā* we find the differentium in a second curve, also shaped like a comma, which is attached to the lower extremity of the right limb. Cf. the form in *āsīd* (in L. 1).

(3) In the case of the short *i*, we find the lower circle or dot of Gupta alphabet of the Western variety, which in Maukharī inscriptions becomes a short vertical curved line, developed at this period into a long curve, which, in two different cases, is shown to be of different lengths.

(4) In the case of *u*, we find the horizontal line at the lower extremity transformed into a curve and elongated. This form continues without alteration till the end of the 10th century A. D., when the first change in its form is found in the Bhagalpur grant of Nārāyaṇapāla.

(5) The rare *o*, becomes an elongated comma laid flat on its back. In the absence of the earlier forms of this letter of the 4th and 5th centuries A. D. comments are impossible. The only known forms are those found in the inscriptions of the Mahārājas of *Uchakalpa* and those of Yaśodharman, which belong to the Southern variety of the Gupta alphabet.

II. Consonants.

(1) For the first time in Eastern India, the first consonant, *ka* always has a loop on its left. The looped form, it should be noticed here, has also been found in the Gañjām plates of the time of Śaśāṅkarāja along with the bipartite form of *ya*. It continued in this form until the loop becomes a semi-circle, in the 11th century A.D.

(2) In *kha*, the triangle at the base of the letter, which is observable for the last time, in the cave-inscriptions of the Maukharīs, becomes transformed into a straight line and a curve. The sides of the triangle become a

semi-circle, while the other side becomes elongated and touches both extremities of the arc. This arc and its base line becomes the right limb, of this letter in the 7th century A. D. The left limb is formed by an increase in the length of the upper hook or curve, which was an open square in Maukharī inscriptions. There is a wedge, instead of a dot or a short straight line at the lower extremity of the left limb.

(3) In the case of *ga*, we find the open square form of the western variety, with its long right limb, again transformed into a curve, with a wedge at the lower extremity of its left limb.

(4) In *gha*, the curvature of the base line, was already observable in the Eastern variety of the early Gupta alphabet. In the sixth century, we see that in the inscription of Yaśodharman, the base line has become a curve on the left side and a slanting line to the right, forming an acute angle with the right vertical. In the Aphsaḍ inscription, we find that, this letter has become something like the tripartite *ya* of the Kuṣāṇa and Gupta periods, the only differentia being the wedges on the top of its three limbs and the presence of an acute angle instead of a right angle, at its right lower extremity.

(5) In *ṅa* we find, the lower right angle is becoming, in some cases, an acute angle and the vertical straight line is transformed into a curve.[1]

(6) In *ca*, the two curves, of the Gupta period, are transformed into a triangle, with a wedge on its apex and a slight elongation of the base line or lower line towards the left.

(7) There is little or no change in the case of *cha* and the ligature *cha* shows that, the older form of *ca* is still being used in certain cases.

[1] Bühler's Indian Palaeography. pl. IV, Col. XIX, 11.

PLATE VI.

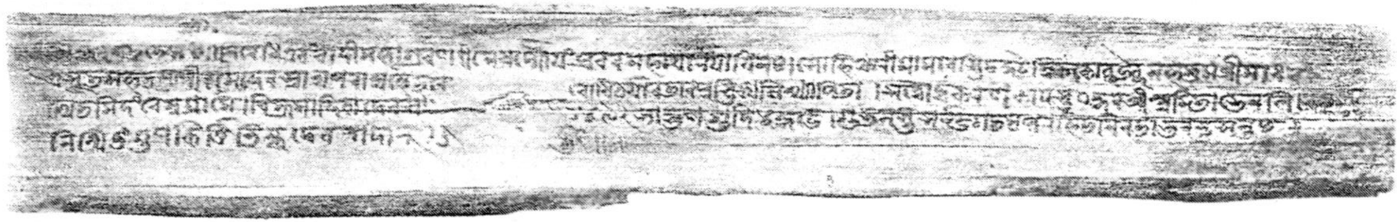

Bodhicaryavatara (Ms. Ga 8067) Fol. 65, Rev. (A. S. B.)

(8) In *ja* the curvature of the lower horizontal line was already perceptible in the Eastern variety form of the early Gupta alphabet. The vertical was also perceptibly curved. Here we find the central horizontal line also curved to the same extent as the base or lower line. A wedge has been added to the right extremity of the upper horizontal line.

(9) There is only one instance of the occurrence of *jha* and it has exactly the same shape which *ma* has in the Allahabad pillar-inscription of Samudragupta.

(10) In the case of *ña,* it occurs in two ligatures, conjointly with *ca* and *ja* ; the form *ñca,* does not differ much from that found in the Allahabad pillar-inscription of Samudragupta, but in the ligature *jñya* its form is still more cursive.

(11) In the case of *ṭa,* we find the Eastern variety differring very much from that of the Western. The *ṭa* in the Aphsaḍ inscription is merely an open curve, with a wedge placed horizontally at the upper end of the curve; but in the Western variety, as in the case of the *Lakkha-maṇḍala Praśasti,* it is a semi-circle with a serif, which is attached to the curve by means of a wedge.

(12) In the case of *ṭha* we find the ancient Maurya form still being used in Northern India without any change.

(13) In the case of *ḍa,* we see that the letter consists of two small curves. In the last line of Aphsaḍ inscription, in the word *Gauḍena,* we find a more archaic form, resembling the one used in the Allahabad pillar-inscription of Samudragupta ; the only difference being a slight shortening of the length. It may be mentioned in this connection that the word *Gauḍa* is found for the first time in Indian epigraphy, in the Aphsaḍ inscription, where it is

stated that the *Praśasti* was composed by *Sūkṣma-śiva*, a native of the *Gauḍa* country.[1]

(14) In the case of *ḍha,* we find the angle changed into a curve. Cf. the form in the inscriptions of Yaśodharman.[2]

(15) In the casė of a *ṇa,* we see that the base line has become slanting, thus forming an acute angle at the right lower extremity, and the left hook has become lengthened. In the case of the ligature *ṇḍa,* the lingual *ṇa* has acquired a distinctly modern form, consisting simply of two curves.

(16) The lower right limb of *ta,* which was already elongated in the Gupta period, becomes slightly curved and we find a wedge at the top of this letter.

(17) In the cese of *tha* occurs only once and its form, there is very indistinct *e.g. vimathito* (L. 7), but here we find the upper part of the letter distinctly broadened. In ligatures on the other hand, we find the older form still prevailing *e.g.* in *stha* in *kumbhasthalī* (L.1).

(18) In *dha,* the small arc has changed into a semicircle.

(19) In the case of *na,* we find that the looped form of the Early Gupta period has changed into one somewhat resembling the modern Nāgarī one The loop has become :—

(*a*) separated from the main body of the letter,

(*b*) smaller in size,

and (*c*) joined to the main body by a short horizontal stroke.

---

[1] An earlier mention is to be found in the Haraha Inscription of Īśānavarman of [V. E.] 611, which has since been discovered.

[2] Bühler's Indian Palaeography, pl. IV, X, 20.

(20) A still more cursive form is apparent in *pa* and the acute angle has become more pronounced. The right limb shows further downward elongation.

(21) In the Aphsaḍ column of Dr. Bühler's plates, *pha* has been omitted but it occurs among the ligatures *e.g.* Col. XIX, 45. It occurs many times and we have it thrice in the 25th line of the Aphsaḍ inscription:—*Sphaṭika*, *sphara* and *sphurat*.

(22) From this time onward we shall have to discard *ba* from the alphabet, as in Northern inscriptions, *va* took the place of *ba* and its occurrence is occasional.

(23) In the Western variety of the early Gupta alphabet, the left hook of *bha* has changed into a solid wedge, and this wedge has developed into a hollow one, at the same time, separating the right limb of the letter from the upper part. So for all practical purposes, the distinction between *ha* and *bha* had ceased.

(24) In *ma* the acute angle, observable in the western variety alphabet of the early Gupta period, develops still more strongly and causes a downward elongation of the right limb.

(25) We find two varieties of *ya* in the Aphsaḍ inscription. In the first place, we have the bipartite form, with a clear acute angle at its lower extremity and in the second place, a later form, in which the acute angle is less prominent, but the downward elongated of the right limb has already assumed a settled from.

(26) In *ra*, we find for the first time, a pointed wedge or arrow-head, at the lower extremity, which is found earlier in inscriptions of the western variety *e. g.* the *Lakkhamandala Praśasti*[1] and the Bodh-Gayā inscription

---

[1] Ep. Ind., Vol. I, p. 12.

of Mahānāman. It is still more developed in the Aphsaḍ inscriptions where it resembles a *ḍa* of short stature.

(27) We find two forms of *la* also. In the first case, the curve or hook in the left limb of the letter has been lengthened downwards with a very slight outward curve at its lowest extremity. In the second case, we find the hook on the curve of the left limb, instead of being prolonged downwards, has acquired an inward length, very much resembling the modern Nāgarī and Bengali forms of the letter.

(28) The triangular *va* of the early Gupta period suffers the same transformation as the triangle at the base of *kha*. Two sides of the triangle are converted into a curve, while the third side is lengthened. A wedge is invariably to be found on the top of the letter.

(29) In *śa*, the upper part of the letter was a curve in the early Gupta alphabet, whether Eastern or Western. In the later western variety it changed to a rectangle. But in the Aphsaḍ inscription, we find, for the first time, the upper part consists of a loop, while the right lower limb has been elongated upwards.

(30) We find three distinct forms of *sa*.—

(*a*) The looped form which occurs in the Aphsaḍ inscription alone (cf. Bühler's tables, pl. IV, XIX, 38).

(*b*) The form in which the loop is changed into a hollow wedge (cf. Bühler's tables, pl. IV, XVIII, 38).

(*c*) In the third variety which is found exclusively in the Shahpur image-inscription of Ādityasena, the apex of the wedge has separated and ceased to be a wedge. This form is found in the 6th and 9th century inscriptions of north-eastern India.

(31) We find one form of *ha*, and the only changes noticeable are the elongation of the curve or hook in the right limb of the letter, and the introduction of the wedge at the top and the slanting of the hitherto horizontal base line.

The next inscription of the Eastern variety is the Deo-Baranark inscription of Jīvitagupta II, the great-grandson of Ādityasena. Most probably, this record was incised in the earlier part of the 8th century A. D. The following inscriptions of Eastern India may be taken as type-specimens for the 8th century A. D. :—

1 The Deo-Baranark pillar-inscription of Jīvitagupta II. We have a certain date for Ādityasena in the Shahpur image-inscription. Three full generations elapsed between him and Jīvitagupta II. If these generations be taken to be short and to have covered fifteen years on the average, we arrive at the 8th century A. D. as the date of Jīvitagupta II. Consequently it may be affirmed that the Deo-Baranark pillar was incised either in the first or the second decade of the 8th century A. D.

2. The Khālimpur grant of Dharmmapāla, the year 33[1].

3. The Bodh-Gayā image-inscription of the time of Dharmapāla, the year 26[2]

It is now quite certain that the reign of Dharmmapāla fell in the 8th century A. D., because he was a contemporary of —

(i) the king Indrarāja or Indrāyudha of Kanauj who is stated in the *Harivaṁśapurāṇa* to have been living in the Śaka year 705 = 783 A. D.,[3]

---

[1] J. A. S. B., 1894, pt. I, p. 53, pl. III.

[2] *Ibid*, (N.S.) Vol. IV, p. 102, pl. VI. ; Annual Rep. Arch. Survey 1908-9, pp. 148-50.

[3] Peterson's 4th Rep. on the Search for Skt. Mss. in the Bombay Presy., pp. XLI and 176 ; Ind. Ant., Vol. XV, p. 141.

(ii) a king named Cakrāyudha, whom he offered the throne of Kanauj, and who was defeated by the Gurjjara-Pratīhāra king Nāgabhaṭa II,

(iii) the Gurjjara-Pratīhāra chief Nāgabhaṭa II, for whom we have a certain date in the Buchkala inscription[1] of V. S. 872=815 A. D.,

(iv) the Rāṣṭrakūṭa king Govinda III[2] whose certain dates range from 794—813 A.D.[3]

The Deo-Baranark inscription of Jīvitagupta II is in a bad state of preservation and the facsimile given in Dr. Fleet's work has not been well reproduced. We find here the forms of initial vowels have not changed. *Ka, ga, ca, ja, ṭa, ṭha, ḍa, da, dha, na, bha, ma, ya,* and *ha* also have not changed. We find changes in the cases of—

(1) *ṇa,* in which we find the right hook or curve further lengthened downwards,

(2) in the case of *ta* also we find a similar increase in the downward length with a very slight, almost imperceptible, curve at its lower extremity,

(3) in *tha,* we find the top of the latter broadened, most probably due to "the elongation of the ends of the wedges and of the use of long straight strokes"[4], cf. *yathā* in (L. 14),

(4) we find two forms of *pa*: (*a*) the older form, in which the acute angle is still prevalent; and (*b*) in which the acute angle, though present, is less remarkable and has given place to a downward elongation of the right vertical line e.g. in the ligature *spa*

---

[1] Epi. Ind., Vol. IX, p. 193.

[2] J. B. B. R. A. S., Vol. XXII, No. LXI, p. 128.

[3] Epi. Ind., Vol. VIII, App. II, p. 3,

[4] Bühler's Indian Palaeography, Eng. Ed., p. 53.

(5) in the case of *la*, we find the acute angle having, in certain cases, become too small and the right vertical straight line produced downwards, e.g. in *kamala* (L. 4), but in other cases, it retains the form of the Aphsaḍ inscription, e.g. *valavī* (L. 6.),

(6) we find two forms of *śa* also :—(*a*) the earlier, with a curved, top as in *paramamāheśvara* (L. 3), and (*b*) the later form, which we find for the first time, and which resembles the 9th century form of the Dighwā-Dubhauli grant,[1]

(7) in *ṣa* the lower part of the left limb is cursive and projects beyond the vertical level of the left side of the letter,

(8) the third variety of the dental *sa* of the Aphsaḍ inscription is used in all cases.

The Bodh-Gayā and Khālimpur inscriptions of the 26th and 32nd year of the reign of Dharmapāla, most probably, were incised in the 9th and last decade of the 8th century A.D.

In the Bodh-Gayā inscription of Dharmapāla we find :—

1 three forms of *śa* :

(*a*) the ancient form with the round top as in *Śilābhidaḥ* L. 1, *Keśava* L. 2 and *ṣaḍ-viṅśati* L. 7,

(*b*) the later form without the cross-bar as in *Mahadevaś-caturmukha and śreṣṭha* (L. 2),

(*c*) the transitional with the lingering cross-bar, as in *śreyase* (L. 4) ;

2 the cross-bar of the lingual *ṣa* going to intersect the acute angle at the bottom, instead of joining the right vertical line ;

[1] Bühler's Indian Palaeography, Eng. Ed., pl. IV, XXI, 36.

3 in *ja* the upper horizontal bar disappearing entirely and being substituted by a wedge. The middle horizontal bar is a curve and longer in size in one case (*mahībhuji* L. 7) and shorter in another (*ujjvalasya* L. 1) ;

4 two forms of *na* :

(*a*) the older looped form occurring in all cases except two,

(*b*) the transitional form, between the Gupta shape and the Nāgarī or Bengali form, which we find in *ahani* (L. 9) and most probably also in *khānitā* (L. 6) ;

5 in *ṇa*, the base line almost disappearing in many cases, as in *puṣkarṇī* and *Viṣṇu* (L. 5) *drammāṇāṁ* and *sahasreṇa* (L. 6), the base line finally perceptible in *putreṇa* (L. 2) ;

6 in *ha*, the acute angle, at the lower extremity, more sharply defined. The characters of the Khālimpur grant of Dharmmapāla appear next, and in it we find some notable changes.

I. *Vowels.*

1. In *a*, we find a broad top-stroke, for the first time, which makes, the resemblance of the letter, to the initial Bengali *a* complete. Cf. *ajani* (L. 45).

2. In *ā*, we find, the length of the vowel is denoted, even in the case of the initial, by a full length vertical straight line, instead of a curve, attached to the lower extremity of the right limb. In the case of the medial, this form is to be found, in all cases, in the Bodh-Gayā inscription also. For the initial form, cf. *asīd* in L. 5.

3. In the case of *i*, we see that the usual form is a wedge at the top with two circular dots below. Cf. the form in *iva* (L. 4) and *iti* (L. 7).

PLATE VII.

The Prapitamahesvara Temple Inscription-Gaya, V. S. 1299.

II. *Consonants.*

1. *Ka* retains the looped form, but the acute angle at the bottom becomes more sharply defined.

2. In *kha,* we find the hook at the top, having become elongated, is converted into a left limb, which in certain cases *e.g.* in the Bodh-Gayā inscription, is projected further downwards than the right limb. In this inscription, the acute angle in the right limb, becomes still more sharp, *e.g. nikhila* (L. 20) and *khalu* (L. 25).

3. In *ga,* we find the left limb has been sharply curved to the right, the extremity of the curve being occupied by the usual wedge.

4. In *gha* we have a broad top stroke, the left end of which is connected with the lower extremity of the right vertical line, by means of two curves. In fact, the base line of the 5th century *gha,* consisting of a curve to the left and a slanting straight line to the right, has been transformed into two distinct curves, while the acute angle at the bottom has become very small.

5. *ṅa* occurs in ligatures only and has not changed, cf. *Saṅgīryamānaḥ* (L. 22).

6. In *ca,* there is no other change, save the sharpness of the acute angle and the consequent decrease in the breadth of the letter.

7. In *cha* also, there is little or no change, except the downward elongation of the vertical line, which forms a short tail, attached to the point or junction of the two circles, cf. *ahavecchā* (L. 20).

8. In *ja,* we find remarkable changes. The lowest horizontal line consists of a hook, while the middle horizontal has been forced downwards ; the place of the upper horizontal line being taken by a wedge. There is very little difference between this form and the modern Bengali form of this letter.

9. *Ña* is to be found in ligatures only, cf. *sarvvaajña* (L. 1) where the reproduction is not very distinct.

10. Another important modification is to be found in *ṭa*, where instead of the semi-circle, we find the letter consists of a top-stroke, a vertical straight line attached to the right extremity, which forms the right limb, and a curve, attached to the left end of the top-stroke, by means of another curve.

11. *Tha* has changed from a circle into a semi-circle with a straight line attached to its both ends and slightly produced downwards, beyond it ; cf. *kaṇṭhe* (L. 23). This form is not to be found in the 9th and 10th century inscriptions.

12. In *ṇa*, we find that in all cases the older form is still prevalent. In no case we find the suppression of the base line, as we do in some cases of the Bodh-Gayā inscription.

13. In *ta*, we find the curve on the right hand having a distinct tendency to become a straight line.

14. In *tha*, we find a more archaic form, as neither the top-stroke nor the broadening of the upper part of the letter is perceptible.

15. In the case of *da*, we find further changes The curve in the middle of the letter has been changed into a sharp acute angle and the slight curve at the bottom lengthened downwards.

16. In *dha*, we find no change, except the sharpening of the acute angle and the consequent shortening of the breadth.

17. Another archaic form is that of *na*, which in all cases, shows the early Gupta looped form instead of the modern one.

18. In *pa*, we find the acute angle has almost disappeared and the letter consists of a top-stroke, a

vertical straight line, attached to its right end a curve attached to the left end of the top-stroke and the lower part of the vertical.

19. *Pha* is denoted by the absence of the top stroke. It resembles a *pa* without the top stroke and a small curve attached to the upper part of the right vertical line, cf. *phani* (L. 15).

20. In *bha*, there is no change beyond the sharpening of the lower angle.

21. In *ma* also there is no change save the decrease in the size of the acute angle.

22. In *ya* the vertical straight line is slightly projected downwards beyond the point of the junction with the curve.

23. In *ra* the arrow-head or the wedge becomes distinct.

24. Another remarkable change is to be found in *la*. The base line of this letter, which became slanting in the inscriptions of the later Guptas of Magadha, has been entirely suppressed in the majority of cases. In this record the hook or curve in the left limb of this letter is attached to the middle of the right vertical straight line by another curve and the letter becomes what it is in modern Nagarī or Bengali. It should be noticed in this connection that the older form is preserved in the sea where the base line is distinct.

25. In *va*, we find a similar downward prolongation of the right vertical straight line.

26. In *sa*, we find the looped form in all cases. The later forms, used in the Bodh-Gayā inscription, are not in evidence.

27. In *śa*, we find the older form, in which the cross-bar touched the right vertical straight line, instead of the later form to be found in the Bodh-Gayā inscription.

28. *Sa* retains the form which we find in the Deo-Baranark inscription of Jīvita-Gupta II without any change.

29. The form of the letter is entirely changed in *ha*, where we find the upper angle changed into a curve and the lower angle replaced by a short vertical straight line. So, the letter now consists of a wedge at the top, a curve below and two short vertical straight lines.

From this point we have to recognise four different varieties in Northern alphabets :—

(i) the Eastern, the development of which, we have to follow, in order to trace the origin of the Bengali script;

(ii) the Central, which gradually developed into the modern Nāgarī and the alphabet of the Southern Punjab and Rājputānā;

(iii) the Śāradā, which according to Bühler, "appears since about A.D. 900 in Kashmir and in the North-Eastern Punjab (Kangra and Chamba);"[1]

(iv) the North-Western. The alphabet has not as yet, obtained proper recognition. It is to be found on the coins of the Hindu kings of Kabul or Ohind[2] and in certain 9th or 10th century inscriptions discovered by Sir Harold Deane, which have not been properly dealt with as yet".[3] It may be termed the Trans-Indus alphabet of the 9th or 10th centuries A.D., which died away after the Muhammedan occupation of the country. It may be noticed, however, that it survived till the earlier part of the 11th century A.D., when we find it on the little known silver coins, with Sanskrit legends, issued by the famous conqueror, Sultan Mahmud of Ghazni.[4]

---

[1] Bühler's Indian Palaeography, Eng. Ed., p. 57.

[2] V. A. Smith, Cat. of Coins in the Indian Museum, Vol. I, p. 246.

[3] J. A. S. B., 1898, pt. I, p. 6, pl. VII 55.

[4] S. L. Poole's, of Orient. Coins in the Brit. Museum, Vol. II. pp. 149-151, pl. VI.

From this point onward, we shall have to confine ourselves to the development of the Eastern alphabet only, and to compare it with that of the central. This, again, will be called Western, from the point of view of our observation, for the sake of better distinction. In the earlier part of the 9th century A.D., the Gurjjara-Pratīhāras founded an extensive empire in Northern India, which extended from Bihār in the East to the Punjab in the West and from the Himalayas in the North to Malwa and Gujrat in the South. In Bengal, Devapāla succeeded Dharmapāla and kept the Pāla Empire in tact. But his successors, Vigrahapāla I and Nārāyaṇapāla, were not so fortunate and we find that the Gurjjara-Pratīhāra emperors wrested Northern and Southern Bihār from them. We know from three different inscriptions that Magadha or Southern Bihār was included in the dominions of the Emperor Mahendrapāla :

1. The Dighwā-Dubhauli grant of Mahendrapāla, V.E. 955=898 A.D.[1]

2. The Rām-Gayā inscription of Mahendrapāla, the year 8.[2]

3. The Guṇeriā image-inscription of Mahendrapāla, the year 9.[3]

The following inscriptions of the 9th century A.D. may be safely referred to the Eastern variety of the Northern class :

1. The Munger grant of Devapāla, the year 32.[4]

2. The Ghoṣrāwā inscription of the time of Devapāla.[5]

---

[1] Ind. Ant. XV, p. 112.

[2] Cunningham's A. S. R., Vol. III, p. 123, No. 13. pl. XXXVII No. 6.

[3] Ibid, p. 124, No. 14.

[4] Asiatick Researches, Vol. I, p. 123 ; Ind. Ant., Vol. XXI, p. 254.

[5] Ind. Ant., Vol. XVII, p. 309.

3. The Bādāl pillar inscription of the time of Nārāyaṇapāla.[1]

4. The Viṣṇupād temple inscription of Nārāyaṇapāla—the year 7.[2]

5. The Bhagalpur grant of Nārāyaṇapāla—the year 17.[3]

6. The Dighwā-Dubhauli grant of Mahendrapāla—V. E. 955.[4]

7. The Ramgayā inscription of Mahendrapāla—the year 8.[5]

Out of these seven inscriptions the Munger grant of Devapāla is of no use for Palæographical purposes, as its original cannot be traced, and it was published by the late Dr. Kielhorn from the eye copy reproduced in the first volume of the Asiatick Researches. The Ghosrāwā inscription is the only record whose characters may be taken to represent the North Eastern alphabet of the earlier part of the 9th century A.D. Dr. Bühler was certainly wrong in placing the alphabets of the Dighwā-Dubhauli grant of Mahendrapāla and the Asiatic Society's grant of Vināyakapāla[6] before that of the Ghosrāwā Inscription.[7] The approximate date of the Ghosrāwā inscription is also wrongly given. It should be 800-900 A.D. instead of 850-950 A.D. Subsequent examination will prove that the Dighwā-Dubhauli grant is later in date than that of the Bhagalpur grant of Nārāyaṇapāla.

---

[1] Ep. Ind., Vol. II, p 161.

[2] Cunningham's A. S. R., Vol. III, pl. XXXVI.

[3] Ind. Ant., Vol. XV, p. 305; J. A. S. B. 1878, Pt. 1, pl. XXIV-XXV.

[4] Ind. Ant., Vol. XV, p. 112.

[5] Cunningham's A. S. R., Vol. III, pl. XXXVII, No. 6.

[6] Bühler's Indische Palæographie—Tafel IV, Cols. XXI & XXIII.

[7] Ibid, Taf. V, Col. VI.

The following characteristics of the alphabet used in the Ghosrāwā inscription may be noted :—

1. In *A* the top stroke has not yet fully developed. There are two distinct wedges on the top of each of the limbs. In addition to these there is a long narrow wedge at the lower extremity of the right limb.

2. In the case of *Ā* also the top stroke has not yet fully developed.

3. The initial short *I* consists of two circles or dots at the top, and a scroll like curve below.

4. *E* has become a right angled triangle in form.

5. *Kha* still shows a wedge at the bottom of the left limb.

6. *Ca* shows an increase in the breadth.

7. *Ja* shows an archaic form in which the central horizontal bar is slightly slanting downwards and lower horizontal bar shows a small curve at the end

8. In *Ṭa* the right limb is not shown and is archaic in form consisting of a semi-circle with a wedge at the upper end.

9. In *Ṇa* the base line has entirely disappeared.

10. *Tha* shows a broadening of the upper part and consists of a loop and a curve with an acute angle at the bottom formed by a side of the curve and the right vertical straight line.

11. *Da* shows a slanting downward stroke at its lower extremity.

12. *Dha* also shows this stroke.

13. *Na* shows the transitional form between the looped one of the early Gupta period and the Nāgarī or Bengali one. The loop has separated from the main body of the letter.

14. *Pa* is very archaic in form. There is no curvature about it and the lower part shows two right angles instead of an obtuse and an acute angle.

15. In *Bha* we see the slanting downward stroke.

16. In *Ma* the loop is still absent.

17. In *Ya* the acute angle has been entirely suppressed and with the exception of the breadth of the lower part of the letter we have the complete Nāgarī or Bengali form.

18. The base line of *La* has been entirely suppressed. The hook or curve on the left is joined to the right limb by a short straight line.

19. In *Va* the acute angle has given place to the elongation of the right vertical straight line.

20. In *Śa* we find a wedge at the botoom of the left limb and the cross bar has become slanting while the right limb is projected upwards.

21. In Ṣ' the base line has again become horizontal, and the cross bar has slanted downwards.

22. In *Ha* also we find a slightly archaic form as the acute angle has not as yet developed into a second downward stroke.

The archaisms found in the alphabet used in the Ghosrāwā inscription may be explained in this manner. The Ghosrāwā inscription represents the true epigraphic alphabet, in which certain letters are more archaic in form than those in the Khālimpur grant of Dharmapāla. The alphabet used in the Khālimpur grant represents the current-hand-script of the later part of the 8th century A. D. and as such shows much later forms than the Ghosrāwā inscription, which being incised on stone is an Epigraph proper of the 9th century.

PLATE VIII.

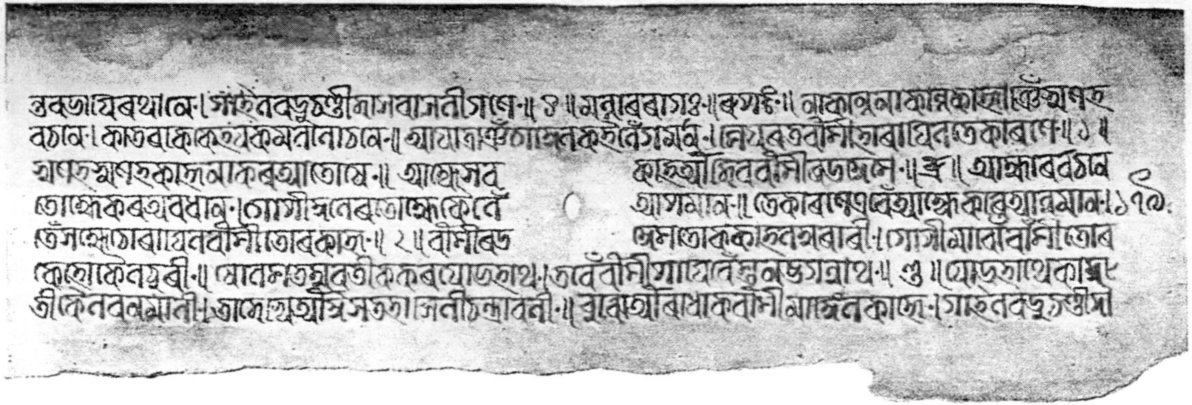

Krsnakirttana (Ms. Bangiya Sahitya Parishad) Fol. 179. Rev.

We pass on to the reign of Nārāyaṇapāla, where we have two stone inscriptions and a copper plate. The Bādāl pillar inscription was found in North Bengal and the Viṣṇupād temple inscription, at Gayā in South Bihār. The copper plate was also found at Bhāgalpur in the latter province. In the case of Epigraphs proper we find that the alphabet of the Bādāl pillar, which is in the East is more archaic than that of the Gayâ inscription of the West. The following points are worth noting in the case of the alphabet used in the Bādāl pillar inscription:—

I. *Vowels* :—

1. The top stroke is prominent in the case of *A* and the letter consists of a vertical straight line drawn downwards from right end of the top stroke. A short straight line stands at right angle to the first one, at its centre, and supports a comma-shaped-curve at its extremity. There is a long thin wedge at the bottom of the vertical line.

2. *Â* is similar in shape, the length of the sound being denoted by a second vertical straight line placed on the right of the first and drawn parallel to it.

3. The initial *I* is denoted by a wedge at the top, and two circles or dots below it.

4. The initial *U* has not changed its form.

5. We find two forms of *E* :—

(*a*) The first one is the triangular form—in which one of the upper angles has gradually become a right angle. The lower part of the letter shows the slightly curved downward stroke.

(*b*) In the second form we find that it has ceased to be a triangle. The hypotenuse has snapped leaving a curve at the top of the vertical side and a part of it at the lower end. The resemblance to the modern Bengali form is now complete. *Cf.* the form in *eva* (L. 13).

II. *Consonants* :—

1. In many cases there is no trace of an acute angle at the lower part of *Ka.* The letter consists of a top-stroke, a vertical straight line with curving end drawn at right angles to the former, and a curve attached to the left side of the vertical, the upper part of which projects out on the right side and is then turned straight downwards.

2. The base of *Kha* still consists of a triangle but the base line is not horizontal. The upper part of the letter which consisted formerly of a curve with a wedge or short straight line at its end now consists of a curve with another much smaller one as its extremity.

3. In *Ga* the curve has a second one attached to its lower extremity and there is a slight tendency of projecting the vertical straight line upwards, beyond the point of its junction with the curve.

4. There is a distinct tendency towards shortage in the breadth of the upper part of *Gha.* The other changes are the introduction of the top-stroke, the raising of the left curve above the level of the right one, the disappearance of the acute angle and the presence of the slightly curved downward stroke at the bottom.

5. *Ca* has not changed.

6. In *Ja* we find a much later form. The vertical straight line has now become a curve while the central bar or horizontal line has become transformed into a long slanting downward stroke. The top-bar has long ago been converted into a wedge.

7. *Ña* is found in ligatures. In one case we find that it resembles the modern Bengali form. *Cf. ñca* in *Kiñcit* (L. 23).

8. We find two forms of *Ṭa* :—

(*a*) The form met with for the first time in Khālimpur grant in which there is a top-stroke, a right limb consisting of a vertical straight line attached to the right end of the top-stroke, and a left limb consisting of a semi-circle which is attached to the left end of the top-stroke by means of another slanting straight line. *Cf.* *Mukuṭāṅkita* (L. 7).

(*b*) The second form consists of a top-stroke and a semi-circle attached to the left end of it by a slanting straight line. The only difference between this form and the first one is the absence of the right limb. *Cf.* *Vikaṭa* (L. 8).

9. *Ṭha* consists of a plain circle up to this time.

10. *Ḍa* is to be found in *Uḍupa* (L. 7) where the angular form is found to have given its place to the archaic cursive one.

11. In *Ṇa* we find that the base line is still intact but the left hook or curve has been transformed into a vertical straight line slightly curving towards the lower end.

12. *Ta* has not changed but we find two different final forms :—

(*a*) *Vidhivat* (L. 10-11).

(*b*) *Kiñcit* (L. 34).

13. There is a perceptible narrowing of the upper part of *Dha*.

14. In *Na* we find the modern Bengali form. The final form has also been used in the inscription. *Cf.* *Śrī-mān* (L. 12).

15. In *Pa* we find a shortening in the breadth of the letter which makes its resemblance to the modern Nāgarī form complete.

16 In *Pha* the left limb consists of a curve which joins the right one at the lower extremity. The right limb consists of a vertical straight line and a hook or curve to the right attached to its upper end.

17. *Bha* has not changed much.

18. For the first time we find that in *Ma* the base line is almost horizontal and there is a loop at the left end of the base line. The acute angle has been entirely suppressed.

19. In *Ya* we also find a shortage in the breadth of the letter, which makes its resemblance to the modern Nāgarī form, almost complete.

20. In *La* we have the archaic form with the slightly curved base line.

21. In *Va* which does duty both for *Ba* and *Va* we find that the acute angle has entirely disappeared and the letter now consists of a top stroke, a vertical straight line at right angles to the above, and a semi-circle attached to the left side of the vertical.

22. We find four different forms of the palatal sibilant:—

(*a*) The looped form in which the lower part of the left limb ends in a wedge. *Cf.* *Śakra* (L. 1).

(*b*) The looped form in which we find a small triangle at the lower extremity of the looped form. *Cf.* *Śarkkarā* (L. 8).

(*c*) The transitional form between the looped form and the Bengali one in which the letter consists of a vertical straight line on the right, to which is attached a curve by means of a very small horizontal straight line. From the left end of this curve, another curve which ends in a wedge, hangs downwards. *Cf.* *Śiva* (L. 10).

(*d*) The modern Bengali form in which there is no top stroke. The letter consists of a vertical straight line on the right with a curved top and a curved line on the left the upper end of which meets the curved end of the right-limb and has a wedge at its base. *Cf.* *Śāṇḍilya* (L. 1).

23. In the lingual *Ṣa* the breadth of the lower part has decreased considerably.

24. *Sa* has not changed at all.

25. *Ha* in all cases shows the later form of the 11th and 12th century Nāgarī or Bengali, in which the downward stroke which had taken the place of the lower acute angle becomes transformed into a curve.

In the Gayā inscription we find that—

1. Initial *I* has two different forms :—

(*a*) Two circles at the top and a scroll at the bottom. *Cf. Iti* in L. 4.

(*b*) A short horizontal straight line at the top and two small circles at the bottom.

2. *Kha* has acquired the modern Bengali form, in which the letter consists of a vertical straight line on the right and the triangle which has now ceased to be so, as the apex has opened out, and the curve at the top. This curve at the top, and the transformed sides of the triangle form a new limb of the letter. The lower part of the curve at the top has again curved slightly inwards making the resemblance complete.

3. *Gha* still retains the acute angle at the bottom. *Cf. Narasiṅgha* (L. 2).

4. In *Ṭa* we find that the vertical straight line on the right has entirely disappeared. *Cf.* the three instances in L. 2.

5. *Tha* continues to preserve its ancient form.

6. We find two forms of *Pa* :—

(*a*) The more ancient form in which the angles still persist as in *Pravala* (L. 2).

(*b*) The comparatively modern cursive form which is more abundant.

7. *Pha* is to be found in ligatures :—

Sphurad-amala (L. 1-2) and *Sphuṭatu* (L. 14).

8. In the case of *La* we find important changes. The base line has disappeared and the letter consists of a top-stroke, a vertical straight line at right angles to it and two small curves joined together which touch the left side of the vertical line.

9. We find two forms of the palatal sibilant *Śa* here also :—

(*a*) The transitional form between the looped one and the more modern form. This particular transitional form is earlier than that to be found in the Bādāl pillar inscription, as here the loop is still present but nestles against the left side of the right vertical straight line. *Cf. Śetu* (L. 12).

(*b*) The other form is more widely used and is same as variety (*d*) of the Bādāl pillar inscription.

We now turn to the alphabet of the Bhāgalpur grant which is the latest record of Nārāyaṇapāla discovered up to date[1] as it was issued in the 17th year of his reign. We find that in the alphabet of this inscription we have the Proto-Bengali forms almost complete :—

I. Vowels :—

1. *A* is the complete Bengali one in which even the short line joining the comma-shaped scroll to the right vertical line is slanting downwards instead of being horizontal as in the Bādāl pillar inscription. *Cf. Asir* (L. 20), *Abhitva*(*ra*)*māna* (L. 35), *Anyāṁs=ca* (L. 36). The wedge has almost disappeared from the lower part of the letter.

[1] The latest inscription of this prince is a votive record incised on the back of a small metal image found at Binar. It records the dedication of the image at Uddaṇḍapur in the 54th year of the reign of that sovereign. This image is preserved in the Luseum of the *Baṅgīya Sāhitya Parishad* of Calcutta.

2. *Ā* also has a similar form—the length being denoted by a second vertical straight line placed to the right of the letter as in the Bādāl pillar inscription. The *A* and *Ā* of the alphabet used in this inscription is almost the same as those used in the modern Bengali alphabet, the only differentia being the short vertical straight stroke in both letters joining the comma-shaped curve with the top stroke.

3. In the case of initial *I* we find almost the same form as in the Bādāl pillar, *i.e.*, the wedge at the top and two circles or dots below it. The wedge however is modified in form, having lost the upper side of the triangle. *Cf. Iti.* (L. 47 and 50).

4. In the initial *U* we find a change after a long time. The letter now possesses a top stroke and the vertical straight line which had remained unaltered since the early Mauryya period now curves sharply to the left. *Cf. Udīcīṇ-āneka* (L. 26).

II. Consonants :—

1. The triangle of *Ka* has become broader.

2. *Kha* shows the cursive Bengali form found for the first time in the Gayā inscription.

3. *Gha* has lost its acute angle, become shortened in breadth at the upper part and the left curve at the base placed on a higher level than the right one. We have a very close approach to the modern Bengali form in this instance.

4. *Ca* also shows a distinct narrowing at the upper part.

5. In *Ja* we find that in some cases the central horizontal bar of the earlier forms, which becomes almost a downward stroke in the Bādāl pillar inscription, transformed into two straight lines, forming an obtuse angle. In other cases this line becomes merely a curve.

6. In *Ṭa* we find that there is a short downward stroke from the right end of the top stroke which may be a relic of the longer stroke of the form used in the Khālimpur grant.

7. In *Ṇa* we find the proto-Bengali form consisting of two short curves joined on to the left side of a vertical straight line.

8. *Ta* has changed its form after a long time. The letter now consists of a top stroke and a vertical straight line at right angles to it and a curve attached to the left side of the latter. The form resembles the Nāgarī one to some extent.

9. In *Tha* the upper curve has become open showing the evolution of the Bengali form.

10. In *Dha* also the upper part of the letter has in many cases opened.

11. The *Na* has in the majority of cases, the archaic looped form but the loop seems to be drooping or bent downwards.

12. In *Pa* the upper part of the letter has narrowed.

13. *Pha* also shows the decrease in the breadth of the upper part of the letter.

14. *Ma* in all cases has the looped form.

15. In *La* we find the final suppression of the base line.

16. The Palatal *Śa* is in all cases of the looped form.

17. We find two forms of the lingual *Ṣa* :—

(*a*) The first is the older form in which the breadth of the letter is the same in the upper as well as in the lower parts: *Cf. Samāyāt-āśeṣa.*

(*b*) The second is that in which the breadth of the upper part is considerably less than that of the lower. *Cf. Samupagat-āśeṣa* (L. 30).

The Bhāgalpur grant, being written in the current hand script, shows forms much later than the Epigraphs proper.

PLATE IX.

The Umga Hill Inscription of Bhairavendra.

the Bādāl pillar and Viṣṇupād temple inscriptions of the time of Nārāyaṇapāla. The examination of the characters of the Dighwā-Dubhauli grant of the Pratīhāra Emperor Mahendrapāla have been included in this paper though it was issued from Mahodaya or Kanauj, because in the first place, the land granted was situated in the *maṇḍala* and *bhūkti* of Srāvasti, in the second place because it was found in the village Dighwā-Dubhauli in the Sub-Division of Gopālganj, in the district of Saran of the Tirhut Sub-division of Bihār, and in the third place because there are many Eastern variety forms in the alphabet used in it:—

1. The narrow *Ca.*
2. The cursive *Ja.*
3. The later *Ṭa* of the Bhāgalpur grant.
4. The Proto-Bengali *Tha.*
5. The looped *Ma.*
6. The transitional *Śa* in which the loop nestles close to the vertical straight line.
7. The late *Ṣa* in which the cross bar slants downwards.

The exceptional forms are those of:—

(1) *A*, (2) *Kha*, (3) *Gha*, (4) *Ta*, (5) *Ṇa*, (6) *Na*.

We have to admit then that the Dighwā-Dubhauli grant shows the use of an alphabet which is a mixture of the Eastern and Western, a fact not to be wondered at the land was situated on a border. In the Ram-Gayā inscription of Mahendrapāla (regnal year 8=C.898 A.D.)[1] we have a similar mixture:—

1. *Śa* is of the transitional form and shows a triangle instead of a wedge at the lower extremity of the left limb.
2. *Ja* shows the downward slanting of the central bar and extreme cursiveness of the lower one.
3. *Pa* still retains an acute angle.

---

[1] Memoirs of the Asiatic Society of Bengal.

4. *Ma* is looped in form but the lower horizontal bar is perfectly so. There is no slanting.

5. *La* shows the horizontal straight line which joins the curve or hook to the right vertical straight line.

6. *Na* is of the looped form.

7. *Ha* still shows an acute angle but at the same time exhibits a downward curve projecting from the lower angle.

Few inscriptions have been discovered in Northern India which can safely be referred to the 10th century A. D. The reason for the absence of records is not far to seek. The period was a very troubled one and saw the fall of mighty empires. The vast fabric of the Gurjjara-Pratīhāra Empire, imperfectly welded together, was rapidly falling to pieces. Family discord, fanned into flame by neighbouring monarchs, rushed the decay of the Gurjjaras of Kanauj. In the far East the ancient Empire of the Pālas was fast crumbling away. The Pālas were between two fires. The Gurjjara-Pratīhāras in the West, and Mongoloid tribes from the North, were doing their best to annihilate them. We have seen that in the latter part of the 9th century *Magadha* (South Bihar) and *Tīrabhūkti* (North Bihar) had been wrested from the Pālas. South Bihar actually formed a part of the Gurjjara Empire. In the North there was a commotion among the Mongoloid tribes of the Sub-Himalayan regions. Perhaps it was the result of a movement among the Nomads of the Trans-Himalayan deserts, the last wave of which reached the Northern barrier of India. The force that was transmitted through the rocky barrier served to dismantle the tall fabric constructed by Dharmmapāla. The Mongoloid tribes, dislodged from their submontane pastures descended into the plains and conquered North Bengal. In 966 A.D. we find a king of Gauḍa, who professed the Brāhmanical faith, but acknowledged descent from a Non-Aryan clan (*Kāmboja*).

There are only three short votive inscriptions and one copper plate grant which can safely be referred to the 10th century A.D. :—

1. The Dinājpur pillar inscription S. 888+78=966 A.D.[1]

2. The Nālandā image inscription of Gopāla II—the year 1.[2]

3. The Bodh-Gayā image inscription of Gopāla II.[3]

4. The Bāngarh (Dinājpur) grant of Mahīpāla I.[4]

The last one is included in this list because :—

1. We know from the Imadpur image inscriptions that Mahīpāla I reigned at least 48 years.[5]

2. We know from the Tirumalai inscription that the Northern conquest of Rājendra Coḷa I was completed before his 12th regnal year *i.e.* 1023-4 A.D.[6]

3. The Sārnāth inscription of Mahīpāla I is most probably a posthumous one. So is the date V. E. 1083= 1026 A.D. The brothers Sthirapāla and Vasantapāla probably finished the work started by Mahīpāla I.

4. There is barely room for two syllables between the words "*Samvat*" and *lguna.* The second of these must be read *Phā,* the first syllable in the name of the month Phālguna and so there can have been only one numeral to express the year.

Consequently we find that the Bāngarh (Dinājpur) grant of Mahīpāla must be assigned to the latter half of the 10th century A.D.

In the Dinājpur pillar inscription we find that :—

1. The upper curve of *Ga* has given place to a straight line from the left end of which hangs a curved line ending

---

1 J. A. S. B. (N. S.), Vol. VIII, p. 619, pl. XV.
2 Ibid, Vol. IV, p. 105, No II, pl. VII.
3 Ibid, No. III.
4 J. A. S. B. 1892, Pt. I, p. 82.
5 Proc. A. S. B. 1881, p. 98.
6 Ep. Ind., Vol. VII, p. 119-20.

in a wedge and from the right end of which hangs a straight line at right angle to it. *Cf. Gīyate* (L. 2).

2. In *Gha* the curves at the lower part have disappeared entirely and the letter consists of a top stroke, a vertical straight line hanging down from the right end of the former, and a loop in the angle formed by these lines, which is joined to the left end of the top stroke and the lower end of the vertical line by two slight curves. *Cf. Ghaṭā* (L. 3).

3. In *Ca* the acute angle is still present but the upper curve has become a horizontal straight line. The letter has also gained in breadth. *Cf. Ca* (L. 1).

4. In *Ja* we have almost the modern Bengali form. The letter consists of a wedge-shaped top stroke, a right limb, the upper part of which is horizontal and the lower part vertical and a left limb, which is as shaped curve. *Cf. Kāmvojanvayajena* (L. 2).

5. *Ña* is perceptible in the ligature *ñja* and there is no difference in it from the modern Bengali form.

6. In *Ṭa* the only remarkable feature is the remnant of the right vertical straight line of the form of the Khālimpur grant of Dharmmapāla. *Cf. Ghaṭa* (L. 3).

7. *Ḍa* is cursive in form and consists of a wedge at the top and a S shaped curve below which is slightly different from the modern Bengali form.

8. *Ṇa* is exclusively Proto-Bengali in form. It consists of a top stroke, a right vertical straight line and two semi-circular curves attached to one another, the right end of the right one of which touches the upper part of the left side of the vertical. *Cf. Mārgganaguna* (L. 2).

9. *Ta* shows the later form consisting of a top stroke, a vertical straight line and a long slight curve attached to the upper part of the left side of the vertical. *Cf. Gīyate* (L. 2).

10. *Tha* has not changed. The upper loop has not become open as yet. *Cf. Varuthini* and *Pramathane* (L. 1).

11. In *Dha* we find an acute angle and an arc of a circle bounded by a straight line which is produced upwards beyond the point of its junction with the upper end of the curve. *Cf. Vidyādharaiḥ* (L. 1).

12. *Na* has the later form consisting of a top stroke, a right vertical line and a loop in the angle joined to the left side of the latter by a short horizontal line. *Cf. Gauḍapatinā* (L. 2—3).

13. *Pa* has the modern Nāgarī form. *Cf. Prāsādo* (L.3).

14. *Va* shows no difference except the presence of the acute angle.

15. In *Bha* we find a change after a long time. The letter consists of a top stroke, a right vertical straight limb, and a long narrow wedge which is joined to the left side of the vertical line. This wedge seems to have been formed by the closing in of the sides supporting the obtuse and acute angles in the older form. *Cf. Bhūbhūṣaṇaḥ* (L. 3).

16. *Ma* shows the looped form in which the lower horizontal line is at right angles to the vertical. *Cf Niramāyı* (L. 3).

17. *Ya* shows the diminution in the breadth of the lower part of the letter. *Cf. Yasya* (L. 2).

18. *Ra* shows a widening of the wedge. *Cf. Durvvār-āri* (L. 1).

19. *La* shows a slightly archaic form in which the line joining the curve to the right vertical is still horizontal and not slanting downwards.

20. There is no difference between *Ba* and *Va*.

21. *Śa* does not occur.

22. In *Ṣa* we find a diminution in the breadth of the lower part of the letter and a slanting cross bar. *Cf*. *Varṣeṇa* (L. 3).

23. In *Sa* the closing in of the sides has caused a fresh formation of the wedge. *Cf*. *Prāsādo* (L. 3).

24. *Ha* shows a top stroke—the transformation of the upper angle into a curve, and the curved line below the lower angle. *Cf*. *Graho* (L. 2).

The Nālandā (Baragaon in the Patna District) image inscription shows :—

1. That in the west the older form of *Bha* was still being used. *Cf*. *Paramabhattāraka* (L. 1), and *Bhaṭṭārikā* (L. 2) and

2. That the later form of *Śa* is used in all cases: *Āśvina*, *Śudi*, *Parameśvara*, *Śrī* (L. 1), and *Śrī Vāgīśvarī* (L. 2).

The Bodh-Gayā image inscription also shows the exclusive use of :—

1. the older form of *Bha*
2. the later form of *Śa* and
3. the later Bengali form of *Kha*. *Cf*. *Khaḍga* (L. 1), *Duḥkha* (L. 2).

In the Bāngarh inscription of Mahīpāla[1] we find the latest form of the 10th century alphabet of the North East. In this inscription we come across the pure Proto-Bengali alphabet for the first time which is further developed in another century. We find that all earlier forms have gone out of use. The points to be noted are :—

1. The initial *i*, still consisting of a wedge at the top, and two dots or circles below. *Cf*. *iv-aiko* (L. 18).

---

[1] Epigraphia Indica, Vol. XIII.

2. The Bengali form of *Kha* in which the cursive left limb joins the right vertical at its lower end as well as at the top. *Cf.* the instances in L. 27.

3. The looped form of *Gha*. *Cf.* the instances in L. 26.

4. The widened form of *Ca*. *Cf.* *Caraṇa* (L. 24).

5. The Bengali form of *Ja* in which the lower curved line is extended upwards and makes the development complete.

6. The older form of *Ṭa* in which the residue of the right vertical line still exists.

7. *Ṭha* shows a wedge-shaped vertical line for the first time. *Cf.* *Pīṭh-opalaṁ* (L. 14).

8. *Ṇa* has the complete Proto-Bengali form.

9. In *Ta* the left end of the curve was already widening in the Dinājpur pillar inscription but in this record it does not show the change.

10. *Tha* does not show the opening of the upper loop· *Cf.* *Pārthivendrān* (L. 58).

11. *Dha* shows the prolongation of the vertical straight line. *Cf.* *Sandadhānaḥ* (L. 2).

12. *Na* shows the slanting cross-bar between the loop on the left and the right vertical line.

13 *Bha* yet shows the older form.

14. *Ma* shows the slanting of the lower horizontal line which joins the loop to the right vertical.

15. *La* shows the developed Nāgarī or Bengali form.

16. *Śa* shows the later form in all eases and we do not find the looped or any of the transitional forms.

17. We fiud the later form *Ha* in which there is a curved line below the lower (now the only) angle.

In the 11th century A.D., we find a fresh development. In Eastern India the gulf between the alphabets used in the Eastern and Western parts have become wider and consequently we find Nāgarī from Benares westwards, and Bengali from Gaya towards the East. We have very few inscriptions of the western variety. The Pratīhāras still lingered at Kanauj, a helpless prey of the Muhammadan invader and the proud *Candella* Rajput. In Bengal the century saw the rise of a new Empire under Mahīpāla I, the invasion of the Southern Conqueror Rājendra Coḷa I, the fight for supremacy with the Cedī kings Gāṅgeya and Karṇṇa, the final break up under Vigrahapāla and Rāmapāla's attempt to recover the lost supremacy.

In the eleventh century A.D. we shall consider the alphabets of four different inscriptions :—

1. The Sārnāth image inscription of Mahīpāla I, V. E. 1083=1026 A. D.[1]
2. The Krishṇa-Dwārika temple inscription of Nayapāla—the year 15.[2]
3. The Tetrāwān image inscription of Rāmpāla—the year 2.[3]
4. The Deopārā inscription of Vijaysena.[4]

Besides these there are a number of records which need not be taken into consideration at present. Of Mahīpāla I we have the Imadpur image inscription of the 48th year and the Bodh-Gayā image inscription of the 10th year.[5] We have another inscription of 15th year of Naya pāla in the temple of Narasiṁha in the compound of the Viṣṇupād at Gayā.[6] We have two certain inscriptions of the reign of Vigrahapāla III :—

---

[1] Annual Rep. Arch. Survey, 1903-4. p. 222, pl. LXIV. No. 4.

[2] Cunningham's A.S.R. Vol. III. pl. XXXVII. J.A.S.B. 1900. pt. I. p. 193 ; Memoirs, A.S.B. Vol. V. p. 77, pl. XXV

[3] J.A.S.B. (N.S.) Vol. IV. p. 109 pl. VII.

[4] Ep. Ind. Vol. II. p. 307. & plate.

[5] Cunningham's A.S.R. Vol. III. p. 122 No. 9.

[6] J.A.S.B. 1900. pt. I p. 190. note 1. Mem. A.S.B., Vol. V. p. 78, pl XXVI.

(1) The Akṣayavaṭa inscri ption of the 5th year[1] and (2) the Āmgāchhi copper plate grant.[2] So also of the reign of Rāmapāla we have the Chandimau image inscription of the 42nd year.[3] But these inscriptions are useless to us as trustworthy facsimiles have not been published or are not easily obtainable. The impression of the Krishna-Dwārikā temple inscription of Nayapāla was obtained after a good deal of trouble through the kind services of Pandit Parameswar Dayal of Gayā.

In the Sārṇāth inscription of Mahīpāla I we find that a mixed alphabet has been used. There is not the slightest chance of the entire alphabet being called Nāgarī, as a comparison with the Benares grant of Karṇṇadeva, the Cedī ruler, would prove at once that the western variety of the North-eastern alphabet was something altogether differe nt.

The following are the peculiarities of the alphabet used in the Sārnāth inscription of Mahīpāla I :—

(1) *Ā* in *ārādhya* and *ī* in *īśāna* (L. 1) have the western variety form. In *Ā* the comma shaped curve in the lower part of the left limb of the letter has lost its knob or head and has acquired the form of a semi-circle.

(2) In *ī* we find that the letter consists of a horizontal straight line above the two dots below and under them a slight curve indicates the length of the vowel Cf. *Īśāna* (L. 1).

(3) We find Eastern variety forms in *Śa, Ha, La, Ṇa.*

(4) *E* in *etāṁ* (L. 2) has the modern Bengali form in which the loop has opened. So also is *Ja.*

---

[1] Cunningham's A.S.R. Vol. III. p. 132-33. Mem. A.S.B. Vol. V. p.81, pl.XXVII.

[2] Ind. Ant. Vol. XXI. p. 97.

[3] Cunningham's A.S.R. Vol. XI. p. 169. Aun. Sep. Arch. Survey India, 1911-12, p.161, pl. LXXII, fig. 8.

The alphabet used in the Krishna-Dwārikā temple inscription of the 15th year of Nayapāla, is the same as that of the Narasiṁha temple inscription of the time of the same king and the Akṣayavaṭa inscription of the fifth year of Vigrahapāla III.[1] With some modifications, it is used in the Satīghāṭ (*Śītalā temple*) inscription at Gayā of the time of Yakṣapāla.[2] Here we find that :—

(1) *A* has the Bengali form, but the short vertical straight line, joining the comma-shaped curve of the left limb, with the top stroke, is still present; Cf. *ajāta* and *ananya* (L. 5).

(2) In *Ā* the length is denoted by a second vertical straight line ; Cf. *ākulaṁ* (L. 15).

(3) There is no change in *i*, Cf. *iva* (L. 1).

(4) In *U* the inward curvature of the vertical line has disappeared giving place to a vertical line slanting, towards the left, at the end of which is a curve which turns back and nearly reaches the level of the top-stroke.

(5) The Nāgarī form of *E* is prevalent in which the triangle has not opened out as yet. Cf. *ete* (L. 8).

(6) The acute angle is clear at the lower end of *Ka*.

(7) We find a top stroke in *Kha*. Throughout this record the Nāgarī form of *kha* is still prevalent.

(8) The upper part of *Ga* now shows a top stroke.

(9) The looped form of *Gha* is used in all cases ; Cf. *Ślāghā* (L. 13).

(10) We find the same form of *Ca* as that used in the Dinājpur pillar inscription of the Śaka year 888.

(11) In *Cha* there is no other change save the downward projection of the vertical line Cf. *cchavi-cchāyaiḥ* (L. 7).

---

[1] Facsimiles of these inscriptions have since been published in my memoirs on the Pālas of Bengal, Mem. A.S.B. Vol. V. pp. 78-82, pls. XXV-XXVII.

[2] Ind. Ant. Vol. XVI. p. 64. Mem. A.S.B. Vol. V. p. 96, pl. XXIX.

(12) In *Ja* we find that the curve to the right, the disappearance of which make the development of the modern Bengali form, complete, still continues.

(13) *Ña* has the fully developed Bengali form and is to be found in ligatures only, Cf. *Kiñ-ca* (L. 3).

(14) *Ṭa* still consists of a top stroke, a right limb which is a short stump of a vertical straight line hanging from the right end of the top stroke, and a left limb, which is a semi-circular curve, the upper end of which is attached to the left end of the top stroke by a short slanting straight line ; Cf. *Paṭala* (L. 3).

(15) In *Ṭha* we find the top stroke Cf. *Pāṭha-kramād* (L. 3).

(16) In *Ḍha* we find that the letter consists of a top stroke and a scroll below ; *prauḍha* (L. 9).

(17) *Ṇa* has the proto-Bengali form, the only special feature being the top stroke Cf. *Bhūṣaṇaḥ* (L. 5).

(18) In *Ta* we find a broadening of the stroke in the extremity of the curve, which has once been noticed in the Dinājpur pillar inscription.

(19) The upper loop or curve of *Tha* has not opened out as yet.

(20) The angle at the back of *Da* has become sharper.

(21) The upward projection of the vertical straight line continues without change, in *Dha*.

(22) *Na* shows the Bengali form in which the line joining the loop and the right vertical straight line is not horizontal but is slanting downwards.

(23) *Pa* has the Nāgarī form, the only exception being the presence of the acute angle.

(24) *Pha* has the Bengali form.

(25) *Bha* shows the formation of the wedge due to the closing in of the sides. The lower extremity of the letter now curves inward and not outwards.

(26) The looped form of *Ma* is used in all cases. The perfectly horizontal position of the short straight line which joins the loop to the right vertical lines shows that the letter belongs to the western variety of the North-eastern alphabet.

(27) In *Ya* we find the formation of the angle in the left limb.

(28) The wedge shaped *Ra* continues without change.

(29) The Bengali form of *La* shows almost complete development.

(30) In *Va* the acute angle is still to be found in the lower part of the letter.

(31) *Śa* shows a distinct top stroke over the two curves in the upper part of the letter.

(32) *Ṣa* shows an angle in the left limb.

(33) In *Sa* we find that the open wedge has become solid.

(34) *Ha* only is archaic in form. It does not show the curved line below the lower angle.

The Tetrāwān image inscription of the 2nd year of Rāmapāla is not in a good state of preservation. We find that in this inscription we have more instances of western forms than of eastern ones of the North-eastern alphabet:—

1. The initial *I* consists of a horizontal straight line and below it two circles or dots.

2. *Ma* has the Nāgarī form, as in the Krishṇa-Dwārkā temple inscription.

3. The scute angle is absent in *Va*.

4. *Bha* shows the older form in all cases.

5. *Ṭha* is more advanced in form, *e.g.* in *gaṭhitaṁ* (L. 2).

We come to the Deopārā inscription of Vijayasena,[1] where we find the modern Bengali alphabet, with certain exceptions in which the development of the form is still incomplete :—

1. *I* where we find that the two circles have become joined together and ellipsoid in form.[2]

2. *U* where the inward curvature of the vertical is still to be seen.[3]

3. *Ka* does not show the acute angle.[4]

4. *Ga* shows a right angle at the top formed by the top stroke and the right vertical straight line.[5]

5. *Na* shows the modern Bengali form in the ligature.[6]

6. *Ca* has the Nāgarī form, the hollow triangle at the lower extremity is still to the left.[7]

7. *Ja* shows the transitional form.

8. *Ṭa* shows the transitional form in which the top stroke and the straight left limb on the right, have combined to form a curve.[8]

9. *Ḍa* still shows the inward curvature of the vertical line as in *U*.

10. *Ṇa* shows the absence of the top stroke that its development is not yet complete.[9]

11. *Da* shows a curve at the back and is transitional in form.[10]

---

[1] Epi. Ind. Vol., I, p. 307.
[2] Bühler's Indian Palaeography, pl. V. XVIII. 3.
[3] *Ibid*, pl. V, XVIII, 5.
[4] *Ibid*, pl. V, XVIII, 10.
[5] *Ibid*, pl. V, XVIII, 12.
[6] *Ibid*, pl. V, XVIII, 14.
[7] *Ibid*, pl. V, XVIII, 15.
[8] *Ibid*, pl. V, XVIII, 20.
[9] *Ibid*, pl. V, XVIII, 24.
[10] *Ibid*, pl. V, XVIII, 27.

12. *Dha* shows the absence of the horn which characterises the modern Bengali form.[1]

13. *Ṅa* shows that the short line joining the loop to vertical line is still horizontal.[2]

14. *Pa* shows the transitional form.[3]

15. *La* has a peculiar form, resembling *La* which is still found in some cases in modern Bengali Manuscripts where *la* is denoted by a dot placed under *na*.

The development is more or less complete in the case of the following letters :—

1. *A* where the line joining the comma-shaped curve to the top stroke has become slanting instead of being perfectly vertical.[4]

2. *Ā* is absent but we can derive it by adding a vertical straight line to the right of *A*.

3. In modern Bengali *E* shows a further elongation of the base line towards the left, than that in the Deopārā *praśasti*.[5]

4. The development of *O* is full and complete.[6]

5. *Kha* shows the modern Bengali form as found in the Bhagalpur grant. The only change needed to perfect it, is the formation of an acute angle at the bottom.[7]

6. The development of *Gha* also is complete, save the elimination of the curve to the right, above the loop and the junction of the upper part of the loop to the left end of the top-stroke.[8]

---

[1] *Ibid*, pl. V, XVIII, 28.
[2] *Ibid*, pl. V, XVIII, 29.
[3] *Ibid*, pl. V, XVIII, 30.
[4] *Ibid*, pl. V, XVIII, 1.
[5] *Ibid*, pl. V, XVIII, 7.
[6] *Ibid*, pl. V, XVIII, 9.
[7] *Ibid*, pl. V, XVIII, 11.
[8] *Ibid*, pl. V, XVIII, 13.

7. *Cha* also is complete. The depression of the circle[1] has given the letter modern form and the opening of the curve to the right at the lower end would complete the development.

8. In *Jha* the upper part of the limb was eliminated later, forming the modern shape.[2]

9. *Ña* occurs in ligatures only[3] but it has the fully developed Bengali form. In fact the modern Bengali form, as has been already shown, developed much earlier.

10. *Dha* has the same form as that to be found in the Krishṇa-Dwārikā temple inscription.[4]

11. *Ta* shows the fully developed form. The hook with the extended head, having become shortened, has the form of a knob. The only change in subsequent centuries was the upward elongation of the curve at the lower extremity of the letter.[5]

12. In *Tha* we find a transitional form[6] which had almost acquired completion. In subsequent centuries we find the elimination of the wedge at the lower extremity of the vertical line and the formation of an acute angle.

13. *Pha* has acquired the modern form about a century ago.[7]

14. In *Bha* we find the almost completely developed form.[8] The only change in subsequent centuries is a curvature of the solid wedge and an upward elongation of the lower extremity.

15. *Ma* shows the complete development.[9]

---

[1] *Ibid*, pl. V, XVIII, 16.
[2] *Ibid*, pl. V, XVIII, 18.
[3] *Ibid*, pl. V, XVIII, 19.
[4] *Ibid*, pl. V, XVIII, 23.
[5] *Ibid*, pl. V, XVIII, 25.
[6] *Ibid*, pl. V, XVIII, 26.
[7] *Ibid*, pl. V, XVIII, 31.
[8] *Ibid*, pl. V, XVIII, 33.
[9] *Ibid*, pl. V, XVIII, 34.

16. In *Ya* the only change needed to complete the development is the formation of an acute angle at the bottom.[1]

17. In *Pa* the solid wedge at the lower extremity,[2] becomes hollow, in fact a triangle, in later years.

18. In *Va* we find a semi-circular curve, which is attached to the vertical line. In subsequent years this again becomes a triangle.[3]

19. The left limb of *śa* has become shortened in length. The only change needed is the formation of two loops at the end of the left limb and the suppression of one of the two curves in the upper part.[4]

20. In *Ṣa* also we find the form[5] almost completed. The only change needed is the formation of an acute angle at the bottom.

21. The final development of the form of *Sa* is to be found in the Deopārā *praśasti*.[6]

22. We find the transitional form of *Ha* in this record. The subsequent changes are the formation of a knob instead of the curve to the left, in the upper part of the letter,[7] and the addition of a top stroke.

In the twelfth century we come across a number of historical events. The Gaharwārs or Gāhaḍavālas made themselves secure at Kanauj. In the East, the power of the Pālas, declined gradually. Their dominions in Bengal were gradually acquired by the Senas, and in Bihār by the Gaharwārs. In this century we find the completion of the

---

[1] *Ibid*, pl. V, XVIII, 35.
[2] *Ibid*, pl. V, XVIII, 36.
[3] *Ibid*, pl. V, XVIII, 38.
[4] *Ibid*, pl. V, XVIII, 39.
[5] *Ibid*, pl. V, XVIII, 40.
[6] *Ibid*, pl. V, 41.
[7] *Ibid*, pl. V, XVIII, 42.

development of the modern Bengali script with exceptions of a few letters such as :—

(1) Ṛ, (2) Ṛi, (3) *ca*, (4) *cha*, (5) *ṭa*, (6) *ṇa*, (7) *bha*, (8) *Śa* and (9) *Ha*.

the final changes in which took place after the Muhammadan conquest of Northern India.

In this century, it will not be necessary to consider ṭhese alphabets used in the different inscriptions, as our narrative of the development of the Bengali alphabet is almost complete. We shall, simply, note the changes in the forms of the letters as they pass through this period. Again, with the extension of the Gāhaḍavāla Empire towards the East the eastern limit of the use of the western variety of the North-Eastern alphabet also extended eastwards in the century. In the Śaka year 1059-1137 A.D. we find the western variety in the Govindpur (near Nawada in the Gayā District) stone inscription of the poet Gangādhara[1] which is now in the Indian Museum at Calcutta. Again in the 4th decade of the thirteenth century of the Vikrama era we find the western variety in the Bodh-Gayā inscription of Jayacchandra.[2] The alphabet of these inscriptions is altogether different from that used in the Deopārā *praṣasti* and other eastern variety inscriptions of the North-Eastern alphabet, so that it is unnecessary to enter into an analysis of it. The further development of the alphabet will be shown from the specimens used in the following inscriptions :—

(1) The Māndā inscription of the time of Gopāla III.[3]
(2) The Kamauli grant of Vaidyadeva.[4]

---

[1] Ep. Ind., Vol. II, p. 333.
[2] Mem. A. S. B., Vol. V, p. 109, pl. XXX.
[3] Proc. A. S. B. 1881, p. 172, pl. VIII.
[4] Epi. Ind., Vol. II, p. 350.

(3) The Torpondighi grant of Lakṣmaṇasena.[1]

(4) The Dacca image inscription of Lakṣmaṇasena—the year 3.[2]

(5) The Bodh-Gayā inscription of Aśokacalla—the *La-saṁ* 51 = 1170 A.D.[3]

(6) The Gadādhara temple inscription of V. E. 1232 = 1175 A.D.[4]

(7) The alphabets used in the Manuscripts of *Pāncākara, Yogaratnamālā* and *Guhyāvalī-vivṛti* written in the 37th, 38th, and 39th year of the reign of Govindapāla, *i.e.*, 1198-1200 A.D.[5]

---

[1] Epi. Ind., Vol. XIII, p. 8.

[2] J. & P. A. S. B., Vol. IX, p. 290, pl. XXIV.

[3] Cunningham's Mahabodhi, p. 78, pl. XXVIII A.

[4] Cunningham's A. S. R., Vol. III, p. 125, pl. XXXVIII; Mem. A.S.B., Vol. V, p. 109, pl. XXVIII.

[5] Bendall's Cat. Skt. Mss. in the Univ. Liby., Cambridge, pp. 188-190, No. 1699, I-III.

CHAPTER IV

The Final Development of the Alphabet.

I. *Vowels*:—

(1) *Ā*:—

(*a*) In the Māndā inscription, the line joining the comma shaped curve to the top stroke, is still intact; and that joining it to the right vertical still horizontal. There is also a long narrow wedge at the bottom. *Cf. Artha* (L. 8).

(*b*) In the Kamauli grant the top stroke has given place to a wedge, at the line joining 'it to the curve being suppressed. The wedge at the bottom has opened at the top.[1]

(*c*) In the Gadādhara temple inscription, which has been very slovenly executed the comma-shaped curve touches the right vertical but the line joining it to the top stroke has not yet been suppressed. *Cf. Anākāri* (L. 6).

(*d*) In the Cambridge Manuscripts the wedge at the bottom and the line joining the comma-shaped curve are still present.[2]

These two were not dropped until the present time. In a Sanskrit inscription written in Bengali characters of Śaka 1666—1744 A.D, found at *Kāmākhyā* in the Gauhati District, Assam, we find that though the wedge at the bottom has disappeared, the line between the curve and the top stroke is still present. *Cf. Āmrātakeśvarasya* (L. 14).

---

[1] Bühler's Indian Palæography, pl. V, XIX, 1.

[2] *Ibid*, pl. VI, X, 1.

2. *Ā* :—

(*a*) The straight line to the right of *Ā*, which denotes the length of the vowel, is joined to the main body of the letter by a short slanting straight line in the Kamauli grant.[1]

(*b*) The wedge is present at the bottom of *Ā* in the Torpondighi grant, and the line joining the main letter to the right hand vertical is not slanting but vertical, in fact a prolongation of the top stroke. The line joining the top stroke to the curve seems to be suppressed. *Cf.* *Āṅgirasa* (L. 41).

(*c*) In the Bodh-Gayā image inscription of the 51st year of the era of Lakṣmaṇasena, the comma has become a semicirlar curve and the line joining the curve to the top stroke is present. The vertical line denoting the length is joined to the main body of the letter by producing the top stroke towards the right. *Cf.* *Ā-caṁdrārkka* (L. 9).

(*d*) In the Gadādhara temple inscription of the time of Govindapāla (?) we find that both the wedge and the joining line between curve and the top stroke, are present. *Cf.* *Ācandrārka* (L. 11) and *Âśvina* (L. 12).

(*e*) The form used in the Cambridge Manuscripts is exactly similar to (*d*).[2]

3. *I* :—

(*a*) The peculiar form of the initial short *I* used in the Kamauli grant is certainly abnormal, as Dr. Bühler has already remarked :— " But the *I* and *Ī* of plate V, 3, 4, appear to be Southern forms; compare plate VII, 3,IV-VI."[3]

(*b*) In the Torpondighi grant the short *I* consists of a top stroke with a wedge at its left end and a vertical straight line drawn downwards at right angles to it from

---

[1] *Ibid*, pl. V, XIX, 2.

[2] *Ibid*, pl. VI, X, 2.

[3] *Ibid*, p. 59.

the right end, two circles below the wedge, and another curve below them. *Cf. iva* (L. 13) and *iha* (L. 55).

(*c*) We find an almost similar form in the Māndā inscription, *viz.*, a wedge at the top, two circles below it, one on each side and finally a comma below them. *Cf. iti* (L. 4).

(*d*) We find the modern Bengali from in the Bodh-Gayā inscription of Aśokacalla. *Cf. iti* (L. 5).

(*e*) In the Manuscripts from Cambridge we have the transitional form, which is the same as that used in the Deopārā *praśasti.*[1]

The changes between the transitional form of the Deopārā *praśasti* and the Cambridge Manuscripts and the final one of the Bodh-Gayā inscription of Aśokacalla are not easy to trace with the materials at present at our disposal, but they can be guessed with a tolerable degree of certainty. First of all the loop on the right in the transitional form became detached to the bottom and was produced below. Then the loop on the left gradually became smaller until it disappeared altogether or became a dot. The right limb then gradually assumed a vertical position. We find the fully developed form in the 15th century in a Bengali manuscript of *Kṛṣṇa-Kīrttana* of *Caṇḍīdāsa* which is certainly not later than the 15th century A. D. *Cf. Kaile* (L. 2). (See photo of fol. 179.)

4. *Ī*:—

(*a*) The initial form of the long *Ī* is very rare. The form used in the Kamauli grant of Vaidyadeva is certainly of southern origin.[2]

---

[1] *Ibid*, pl. VI, X, 3.

[2] *Ibid*, pl. V, XIX, 4.

(*b*) The length of the vowel is denoted in the Cambridge Manuscripts by a slanting straight line placed below the short *I.*[1]

5. *U*:—

(*a*) The form used in the Kamauli grant shows a hollow wedge instead of the top-stroke, the inward curvature of the vertical line, and the shortness of the terminal curve.[2]

(*b*) The form of the letter in the Torpondighi grant is not much different. Here the top stroke is a very short horizontal line instead of the wedge. *Cf.* *ubhan* (L. 51).

(*c*) In the Cambridge Manuscripts we find the development almost complete. The only change needed is the addition of the curve placed in the modern form above the top stroke.[3]

This stroke we find for the first time in a Bengali Manuscript of Śāntideva's *Bodhi-caryāvatāra* written at Veṇugrāma in the Burdwan District in V.E. 1492=1435 A.D. which was discovered by Mahāmahopādhyāya Hara Prasāda Śāstrī, C.I.E., in Nepal. We find this *U* in L. 1 of the last page (66) in the word *Koccha-uccha.*

6. *Ū* is of very rare occurrence and is to be found in the Cambridge Manuscripts only where we find that the length is denoted by the addition of a second curve at the bottom.[4] The only addition in later periods was the curved stroke above the base line which seems to have been made about the same time as that in the short one.

7. *Ṛ* is, also, of very rare occurrence and we find it for the most part in manuscript records :—

(*a*) It occurs in the Kamauli grant, where it consists of a triangular *va*, with a wedge for its top stroke and a

---

[1] *Ibid*, pl. VI, X, 4.

[2] *Ibid*, pl. V, XIX, 5.

[3] *Ibid*, pl. VI, X, 5.

[4] *Ibid*, X, 6.

vertical straight line to the right, which is joined to the main body of the letter by a slanting straight line.[1]

(*b*) It is of course to be found in the Cambridge Manuscripts where we find the wedge transformed into a top stroke.[2]

In later periods the triangle, in the left limb, opens at the top, and finally a curve is added to the top of the open side. The right limb decreases in length and mounts upwards.

8. *Ṛi* is very seldom found. We find it in the Cambridge Manuscripts, where it is formed by adding a short curve to the foot of the short *Ṛ*.[3] In later times the addition which denotes the length of the vowel becomes angular.

9. *L* is to be found in the Cambridge Manuscripts only where it is a reversed S.[4]

10. *Li* is also to be found in the Cambridge Manuscripts where the length is denoted by the addition of a curve placed below.[5]

The very rare occurrence of *L* and *Li* makes it impossible to trace the later changes in their forms.

11. In *E* the Bengali form was developed long ago and this was continued without change :—

(*a*) In the Māndā inscription in *eva* (L. 7).

(*b*) In the Kamauli grant.[6]

(*c*) In the Madanapāḍa grant of Viśvarūpasena,[7] in *etasmat* (L. 4).

---

[1] *Ibid*, pl. V, XIX, 7.

[2] *Ibid*, pl. VI, X, 7.

[3] *Ibid*, X, 8.

[4] *Ibid*, X, 9.

[5] *Ibid*, X, 10.

[6] *Ibid*, pl. V. XIX, 7.

[7] B.986 A.J. pt. p. I.S. 1. 9, pl. I.

(*d*) In the Bodh-Gayā inscription of Aśokacalla in *eva* (L. 2).[1]

(*e*) In the Gaya inscription of the Gadādhara temple in *eva* (L. 8).[2]

(*f*) In the Cambridge Manuscripts.[3]

12. *Ai* is of very rare occurrence and is to be found in its initial form in the Cambridge Manuscripts only where we find the complete Bengali form.[4]

13. *O* :—

(*a*) It occurs in the Naihāṭī grant of Vallālasena[5] *Cf. Ovāsu* (L. 17).

(*b*) and as a matter of course in the Cambridge Manuscripts.[6]

14. The initial form of *Au* is, also, of very rare occurrence. It is to be found in the Cambridge Manuscripts.[7] The only change in the later periods is the elimination of the lower part of the left limb.

15. *Aṁ* shows the modern Bengali form :—

(*a*) in the Kamauli grant ;[8]

(*b*) in the Cambridge Manuscripts.[9]

In other records the *anusvāra* is a dot or a circle placed on the line :—

(*a*) The Bodh-Gayā inscription of Aśokacalla.

(*b*) The Gadādhara temple inscription.

(*c*) The Torpondighi grant.

---

1 Epi. Ind., p. XXVIII

2 Mem. A. S. B., Vol. V. p., 109, pl. XXVIII.

3 Bühler's Indian Palæography, pl. VI, X, 11.

4 *Ibid.* pl. X, 12.

5 Baṅgīya-Sāhitya Pariṣad-Patrikā, Vol. XVI, p. 238.

6 Bühler's Ind. Palæographie, pl. VI, X, 13.

7 *Ibid*, X, 14.

8 *Ibid*, pl. V, XIX, 38.

9 *Ibid*, pl. V, X, 15.

PLATE X.

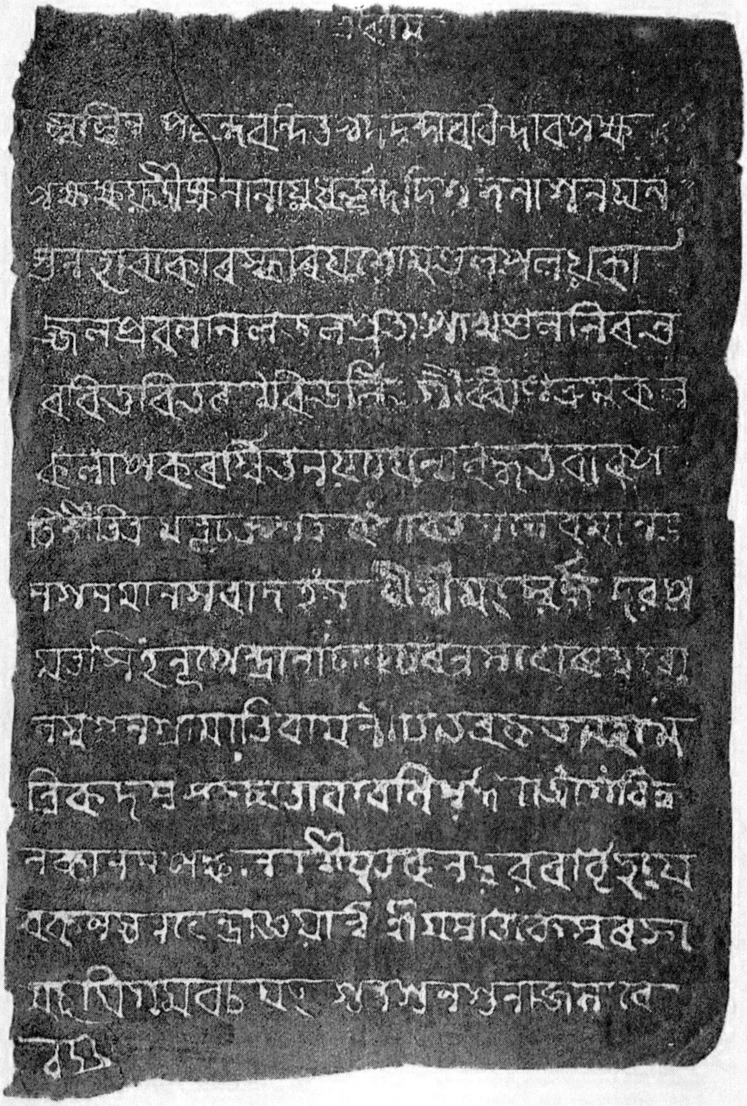

Kamakhya Hill Inscription of Pramatha Sinha-Saka 1666.

16. *Aḥ* shows the old form even in modern Bengali. It has the form of 8 in the Dacca inscription,[1] *pratiṣṭhite-tiḥ* (L. 2) and in the Cambridge Manuscripts.[2]

II. *Consonants.* :—

1. *Ka* :—

(*a*) In the Kamauli grant we find the older form of *ka* in which the acute angle at the bottom has not reappeared.[3]

(*b*) The reappearance of the acute angle is to be observed in :—

(*i*) The Māndā inscription.[4]

(*ii*) The Torpondighi grant.[5]

(*iii*) The Dacca image inscription.[6]

(*iv*) The Bodh-Gayā inscription of Aśokacalla.[7]

(*v*) The Gadādhara temple inscription at Gayā.[8]

But in these records the left limb or back of the letter remains cursive. The angularity of this part, which shows that the development is final is to be found in the Cambridge Manuscripts.[9]

2 The development of *Kha* was almost complete in the 11th century A.D. In this century we see that in the majority of cases, with the appearance of the acute angle at the bottom the development is complete :—

(1) In the Kamauli grant.[10]

---

[1] J. and P. A. S. B., Vol. IX, p. 290, pl. XXIV.

[2] *Ibid*, pl. VI, X, 51.

[3] *Ibid*, pl. V, XIX, 10.

[4] Mem. A. S. B., Vol. V, p. 102, pl. XXX.

[5] Epi. Ind., Vol. XII

[6] J. & P. A. S. B., Vol. IX, p. 290, pl. XXIV.

[7] Epi. Ind., Vol. XII,

[8] Mem. A. S. B., Vol. V, p. 109, pl. XXVIII.

[9] *Ibid*, pl. VI, X, 15.

[10] *Ibid*, pl. V, XIX, 11.

(2) In the Torpondighi grant in *Khalu* (L. 22).

(3) In the Gadādhara temple inscription in *Bhikho-deva* (L. 11).

(4) in the Cambridge Manuscripts.[1]

The only exception is the Bodh-Gaya inscription of Aśokacalla, in *Lakhvaṇa* (L. 12).

3. In *Ga*, the only change needed, was the elimination of the right angle, at the right end of the top stroke and the substitution of a curve for it, as well as the upward elongation of the vertical line :—

(*a*) In the Māndā inscription we find in one case that the right angle is still present, *parabhāgo* (L. 1) and in another that the transformation has taken place *Śrīmadgopāla* (L. 3).

(*b*) The transformation is complete in the case of the Kamauli grant.[2]

(*c*) The Torpondighi grant shows the retention of the right angle.

(*d*) The letter is incomplete in *Gurava* (L. 5) of the Bodh-Gayā inscription of Aśokacalla, though the right angle has disappeared.

(*e*) The Gadādhara temple inscription shows both forms. *Cf.* *Govindapāla* (L. 3) and *gatarājye* as well as *Gayāyāṁ* (L. 4).

(*f*) The Cambridge Manuscripts show the completely developed form.[3]

4. *Gha* :—

(*a*) In the Kamauli grant the development is not yet complete.[4]

---

[1] *Ibid*, pl. VI, X, 16.

[2] Indische Palæographie, pl. V, XIX.

[3] *Ibid*, pl. VI, X, 17.

[4] *Ibid*. pl. V. XIX. 13.

(*b*) The Torpondighi grant shows an improvement, as the left limb is a curve to the left and not to the right when it touches the top stroke. *Cf. Kṣettr-angha* (L. 10-11).

(*c*) We find the development completed in the Bodh-Gayā image inscription of Aśokacalla, *e.g.*, *Rāghava* (L. 7) *Simghala* (L. 9-10) and *Saṁgha* (L. 10).

(*d*) The development is also shown to be completed in the Gadādhara temple inscription at Gayā. *Cf. lagh* (*v*)*ī* (L. 8) *Rāghavaḥ* (L. 10).

(*e*) The Cambridge Manuscripts show the use of the transitional form, which is almost similar to the form used in the Kamauli grant.[1]

5. *Ṅa* is very rare in use and its initial form cannot be found at all.

6. *Ca* is one of the letters the development of which was completed long after the Muhammadan conquest of the country.

(*a*) In the Māndā inscription *Ca* consists of a wedge as the top stroke, a vertical straight line at right angles to it and a curve to the left, semi-circular in shape, the ends of which touch the vertical line. This is in fact a modification of the *Ca* of the Deopārā *praśasti*. *Cf. vīcī* and *viracita* (L. 1).

(*b*) In the Kamauli grant the letter is almost similar where we find an angle in the curve.[2]

(*c*) The form used in the Torpondighi grant is almost the same as that in the Dinājpur pillar inscription and the Deopārā *praśasti* ; *Cf. Cakra* (L. 4).[3]

(*d*) The form used in the Dacca inscription shows the next state of transition, where the letter consists of a top

---

[1] *Ibid*, pl. VI, X, 18.

[2] *Ibid*, Tafel V, XIX, 15.

[3] *Ibid*, XVIII, 15.

stroke, the vertical line which curves to the left, and a second inward curve joins the lower end of the vertical to the point of its junction with the top stroke. *Cf. Caṇḍīdevī* (L. 2).[1]

(*e*) The same form is used in the Bodh-Gayā image inscription of Aśokacalla. *Cf. ācandrār-kkaṁ* (L. 9).[2]

(*f*) The Gadādhara temple inscription of Gayā shows the use of the same form.; *Cf. caturddaśa* (L. 4).[3]

(*g*) There is no change in the form of the letter in the Cambridge Manuscripts.[4]

(*h*) In the Bengali manuscript of the *Bodhicaryāvatāra* we find the next transitional form. The form used in the word *Bodhicaryāvatāra* (L. 2 of fol. 66) shows that the straight part of the vertical has become a curve, which has swollen out on the right side and not on the left. Consequently the left curve has almost become a vertical straight line.

(*i*) In the next stage we find that the left limb is only slightly curved, while the former vertical line has become very much cursive and has swollen out to the right. *Cf. Caṇḍīdāsa* (L. 1) in fol. 179 of Caṇḍidāsa's *Kṛṣṇakīrttana.*

The next stage is the conversion of the left limb into a vertical straight line, an event which happened sometime after the 15th century A. D.

7. *Cha* is not of common use and is very often to be found in ligatures :—

(*a*) In the Kamauli grant we find the same form as that used in the Deopārā *praśasti.*[5]

---

[1] J. and P.A.S.B., Vol. IX, p. 290, pl. XXIV.

[2] Epi. Ind., Vol. XII, p.

[3] Mem. A.S.B., Vol. V, p. 109, pl. XXVIII.

[4] *Ibid*, pl. VI, X, 20.

[5] *Ibid*, pl. V, XIX, 16.

(*b*) We find the same form in the Torpondighi grant. *Cf*. *Duṣkhacchid-ātyantikī* (L. 4) and *Catuhsīṁ-āvacchinna* (L. 35).[1]

(*c*) There is no change in the form to be found in the Cambridge Manuscripts.[2]

(*d*) The modern Bengali form is to be found in the Bengali manuscripts of the *Bodhicaryāvatāra* written in V. S. 1492 in the word *Koccha-uccha* (L. 1) of fol. 66.

8. *Ja* :—

(*a*) The form of *Ja* used in the Māndā inscription is transitional. *Cf*. *rmmañjarī-piṁjarīsu* (L. 3.)[3]

(*b*) The Kamauli grant shows the fully developed western variety form, with a wedge for its top stroke.[4]

(*c*) In the Torpondighi grant we find another transitional form in which the vertical has not as yet become perfectly straight. *Cf*. *Mahārājādhirāja* (L. 23) but the fully developed Bengali form is also to be found, *Cf*. *Srīmaj-Jayaskandhāvārāt* (L. 23).[5]

(*d*) We find the transitional form in the Bodh-Gayā inscription of Aśokacalla. *Cf*. *Mahārāja* (L. 3) and *Rājānaṁ* (L. 6).[6]

(*e*) The same form is to be found in the Gayā inscription of the Gadādhara temple. *Cf*. *Kāja* (L. 15).[7]

(*f*) The form used in the Cambridge Manuscripts shows the shortening of the right limb.[8]

---

[1] Epi. Ind., Vol. XII, p. 8, pl.

[2] *Ibid*, pl. VI, X, 21.

[3] Mem. A.S.B., Vol. V, p. 102, pl. XXX.

[4] *Ibid*, pl. V, XIX, 17.

[5] Epi. Ind., Vol. XII, p. 9.

[6] *Ibid*, p. 29.

[7] Mem. A.S.B., Vol. V, p. 109, pl, XXVIII.

[8] Indische Palæographie, Tafel VI, Vol. XI, 22.

(*g*) In the Bengali manuscript of the *Bodhicaryāvatāra* we find the Bengali form, the only difference being the shortness of the right limb. *Cf. Kuje* (L. 3) of fol. 66.

The full development of this letter also was completed after the 15th century A. D.

(*h*) The completely developed form is to be found in the Kāmakhyā minor temple inscription of the Śaka 1666=1744 A. D. in L. 4; in the word *Kajjala*.

9. *Jha* is to be found very seldom.

(*a*) In the Kamauli grant its form is very peculiar.[1]

(*b*) The letter does not occur in the Cambridge Manuscripts.

10. *Ña* :—

(*a*) In the Māndā inscription this letter is used in ligatures where it has the peculiar form of initial *E*, the loops on the right being absent. *Cf. Kṛtajña* (L. 6).

(*b*) In the Kamauli grant we have the finished Bengali form in the ligature *ñcai*.[2]

(*c*) The complete form is also to be found in the Bodh-Gayā inscription of Aśokacalla in *jñāna* (L. 4).

(*d*) In the Gadādhara temple inscription at Gayā, the form of the ligature *ñca* is the same as that used in the modern Bengali alphabet. *Cf. mulañca* (L. 8) and *pañcakaṁ* (L. 14).

(*e*) In the Cambridge Manuscripts the form is entirely different, which may be due to western influence.

11. *Ṭa* :—

(*a*) In the Māndā inscription of this letter consists of a wedge as the top stroke and scythe-shaped curve below it. *Cf. Koṭīra* (L. 2).

(*b*) In the Kamauli grant *Ṭa* "seems to have been produced by an abnormally strong development of a

[1] *Ibid*, pl. V, XIX, 18.

[2] *Ibid*, pl. V, XIX, 19.

'Nepalese hook' with a serif at the end, placed above the ancient round *ta* which is represented by the second lower curve on the left."[1] But the form seems to have been developed independently from that used in the Khālimpur grant of Dharmmapāla.

(*c*) In the Torpondighi grant we find a transitional form, consisting of a curve joined to the top stroke by a second one on the left side, and another joined to the right side of the top stroke. *Cf. Mahākṣapaṭalika* (L. 27).

(*d*) The form used in the Bodh-Gayā inscription is peculiar and is formed from the western variety. *Cf. bhaṭṭa* (L. 7).

(*e*) The development is complete in the 15th century when we find the modern form *kuṭumbika* (L. 1) of fol. 66, of the Bengali manuscript of *Bodhicaryāvātāra.*

(12) *Ṭha* :—

(*a*) In the Kamauli grant the development is not clear as the letter is found in the ligature *ṇṭha.*[2]

(*b*) The form in the Torpondighi grant is not clear for the same reason. *Cf. anuṣṭhayine* (L. 42).

(*c*) The archaic form of the Mauryya period is used in the Gadādhara temple inscription of Gayā. *Cf. Gadābhṛṇ-mathe* (L. 7).

(*d*) The modern form is to be found in the Cambridge Manuscripts in the ligature *ṣṭha*[3] but the older form continued to be used till at least the 15th century as we find it in the Bengali manuscript of the *Bodhicaryāvatāra. Cf. Ṭhakura* (L. 2) of fol. 66.

---

[1] *Ibid*, p. 59.

[2] *Ibid*, pl. V, XIX, 21.

[3] *Ibid*, pl. VI, X, 26.

13. *Da* :—

(*a*) The Māndā inscription shows the transitional form in which the curve at the end has not fully developed. *Cf. Aiḍadeva* (L. 6) and *Krīḍati* (L. 7).

(*b*) The Kamauli grant shows the use of the older form in which the vertical line has got a curve to the left in its middle.[1]

(*c*) We find a similar form in the Torpondighi grant in *nicaḍahāra* (L. 33).

(*d*) The Dacca inscription shows the finally developed Bengali form in the ligature *ṇḍi* in *Caṇḍī* (L. 2).

(*e*) In the Bodh-Gayā inscription of the time of Aśokacalla we find the modern form of the ligature *ṇḍa* in *Paṇḍita* (L. 5).

(*f*) We find by the partly complete form of this letter in the Gadādhara temple inscription of Gayā in *Dallano* (L. 6) ; and *Śoḍaś-aiva* (L. 8).

The only change needed to complete the development is the lengthening of the curve at the foot of the vertical straight line.

14. *Ḍha* is also rarely met with :—

(*a*) In the Kamauli grant it has the form of a *Ṭa* of the Māndā inscription.[2]

(*b*) In the Torpondighi grant we find the letter two or three times ; *uttarāḍhā-vāpa* (L. 36) *bhumy-āḍhā* (L. 33) and in these cases we have the same form as that in the Kamauli grant.

The extreme rarity of this letter makes it difficult for us to trace the changes in it. The only change needed is the straightening of the curve to the left.

---

[1] *Ibid*, pl. V, XIX. 22.

[2] *Ibid*, XIX, 23.

15. *Ṇa* is one of those letters in which the development was not complete till the 15th century A.D. In most of the inscriptions we find the Proto-Bengali forms which resembles the modern Bengali letter *la* minus the top stroke :—

(*a*) In the Māndā inscription where the letter is a curve with a straight line on the right and a small vertical line bisecting the curve. This form is the precursor of the modern Bengali form.

(*b*) In the Torpondighi grant.

(*c*) In the Kamauli grant where the vertical line is projected slightly beyond the point of its junction with the left limb.

(*d*) In the Dacca image inscription.

(*e*) In the Bodh-Gayā inscription of Aśokacalla.

(*f*) In the Gadādhara temple inscription of Gayā.

(*g*) In the Cambridge Manuscripts.

(*h*) In the Bengali manuscript of the *Bodhicaryāvatāra* written in 1435 A.D.

The final development is very clearly shown in the Bengali manuscript of Caṇḍīdāsa's *Kṛṣṇakīrttana* where on fol. 179 we find both the transitional and final forms. The transitional form between the Proto-Bengali one and the final Bengali form is the one in *gaṇe* and *suṇaha* in L. 1 where the bisecting vertical line in the curve of the Māndā inscription, seems to have become a horizontal cross bar. The final form shows the elimination of this cross bar in *Suṇaha,* L. 3.

16. *Ta* :—

(*a*) In the Māndā inscription we find the transitional form in which the left limb is curved and the broadening of the top is changed into a knob. The only difference between this form and the Proto-Bengali one is the curvature of the right limb, which in this one turns to the right and not to the left.

(*b*) In the Kamauli grant the Proto-Bengali form is used but the knob is absent.[1]

(*c*) Torpondighi grant shows a further development, *viz.*, : the lengthening of the right curve.

(*d*) The same form is used in the Dacca image inscription.

(*e*) The Bodh-Gayā inscription of Aśokacalla shows the transitional form of the Kamauli grant.

(*f*) This is also the case of the Gadādhara temple inscription of Gayā.

(*g*) The final development is to be found in the Cambridge Manuscripts.[2]

17. *Tha* :—

(*a*) The Māndā inscription shows the use of the archaic form in which the upper loop has not as yet opened out. *Cf. prathita* (L. 4).

(*b*) The Kamauli grant shows the use of the modern Bengali form.[3]

(*c*) In the Torpondighi grant we find the transitional form. *Cf. itham* (L. 36).

(*d*) The fully developed modern Bengali form is to be found in the Bodh-Gayā inscription of Aśokacalla. *Cf. Tathā* (L. 1).

(*e*) The Cambridge Manuscripts also show the modern form.[4]

---

[1] *Ibid*, pl. V, XIX, 25.

[2] *Ibid*, pl. VI, X, 30.

[3] *Ibid*, pl. V, XIX, 26.

[4] *Ibid*, pl. VI, X, 31.

18. *Da* :—

(*a*) In the Māndā inscription the older form with the curved back.

(*b*) In the Kamauli grant we find the same form.[1]

(*c*) The same form is to be found in the Dacca Image inscription along with the completely developed modern form. For the older form see *deva* (L. 2) and for the modern one see *Dāmodra* (L. 1).

(*d*) The Torpondighi grant shows the use of the older form.

(*e*) We find the modern Bengali form in all cases in the Bodh-Gayā inscription of Aśokacalla. But in the Bodh-Gayā inscription of Aśokacalla's brother, Daśaratha, incised in *La-saṁ* 74=1193 A.D. we find the older form in all cases.[2]

(*f*) This is also the case with the Gadādhara temple inscription of Gayā ; *Cf. Govindapāla* (L. 3) and *Dvivedaḥ* (L. 5), but the older form persists in ligatures, *e.g.*, *nda* in *Govinda* (L. 3) and *rdda* in *caturddaśa* (L. 4).

(*g*) The Cambridge Manuscripts show the use of the older form.[3]

19. *Dha* :—

(*a*) In the Māndā inscription we find the use of the older form in which the slanting straight line has not as yet been added to the top ; *Pādadhuli* (L. 4).

(*b*) In the Kamauli grant we find that this addition has already been made.[4]

---

[1] *Ibid*, pl. V, XIX, 27.

[2] Baṅgīya Sāhitya Pariṣad Patrikā, Vol. XVII, p. 216.

[3] Bühler's Ind. Palæographie, pl. VI, X, 32.

[4] *Ibid*, pl. V, XIX, 28.

(c) In the Torpondighi grant we find the fully developed form. *Cf. Indrāyudhaṁ* (L. 1).

(d) This is the case in the Dacca image inscription. *Cf. Adhikṛta* (L. 1).

(e) The Bodh-Gayā inscription of Aśokacalla shows the use of the older form the only exception being that in *Dharmma* (L. 1).

(f) In the Gadādhara temple inscription of Gayā the modern form is used in all cases.

(g) The Cambridge Manuscripts show the use of the older form.[1]

20. *Na* :—

(a) The Māndā inscription shows the modern form with a wedge for its top stroke.

(b) The peculiar form of the Kamauli grant is due to a defect in the facsimile—the line joining the knob to the right vertical, being faint, has not come out well.[2]

(c) The modern form is to be found in all cases in the Torpondighi grant.

(d) This is also the case with the Dacca image inscription.

(e) The same form is used in the Bodh-Gayā inscription of Aśokacalla.

(f) This is also the case in the Gadādhara temple inscription of Gayā.

(g) The Cambridge Manuscripts clearly exhibit the use of the modern form.[3]

---

[1] *Ibid*, pl. VI, X, 33.

[2] *Ibid*, pl. V, XIX, 29.

[3] *Ibid*, pl. VI, X, 34.

21. *Pa* :—

(*a*) We find a transitional form in the Māndā inscription in which the acute angle has reappeared and in which the curve in the left limb has a short inward curve. *Cf.* *Srīmad-Gopāla* (L. 3).

(*b*) This inward curve in the outwardly curving left limb is still more pronounced in the Kamauli grant.[1]

(*c*) The same form is used in the Torpondighi grant.

(*d*) The Dacca image inscription shows the use of the modern Bengali form for the first time in 1122 A.D. (*i.e.*, year 3 of the *Lakṣmaṇasaṁvatsara*). *Cf.* *Pratisthitetiḥ* (L. 2).

(*e*) The modern form is used in all cases in the Bodh-Gayā image inscription of Aśokacalla.

(*f*) The Gadādhara temple inscription of Gayā shows the use of the older form. The influence of the western variety may also be looked for in this case.

(*g*) The Cambridge Manuscripts show the use of the transitional form of the Torpondighi grant.[1]

22. *Pha* :—

(*a*) The Kamauli grant shows a peculiar form which has nothing in common with the modern Bengali one, which latter is angular and was fully developed in the 11th century A. D.[2]

(*b*) The transitional cursive form is used in the Torpondighi grant. *Cf.* *phaṇi* (L. 1).

(*c*) The form used in the Bodh-Gayā inscription of Aśokacalla is very slovenly incised, but it is the modern Bengali form. *Cf.* *phala* (L. 5).

---

[1] *Ibid*, pl. VI, X, 35.

[2] *Ibid*, pl. V. XIX. 31.

(*d*) The modern form is used in the Gadādhara temple inscription of Gayā. *Cf.* *phalaṁ* (L. 13).

23. *Ba* need not be discussed separately as its form is the same as that of *Va*.

24. *Bha* :—

(*a*) The archaic form is used in the Māndā inscription. *Cf.* *parabhago* (L. 1).

(*b*) This is also the case of the Kamauli grant.[1]

(*c*) The same form is used in the Torpondighi grant.

(*d*) This is the form to be found in the Dacca image inscription. *Cf.* *labhrādakanā* (L. 2).

(*e*) The modern form is met with again in the Bodh-Gayā inscription of Aśokacalla.

(*f*) The same form (modern) is used in all cases in the Gadādhara temple inscription of Gayā.

(*g*) The Cambridge Manuscripts show the further development of the modern form.[2]

(*h*) The completed development is shown in the Bengali manuscript of the *Bodhicaryāvatāra*, *Śobhābhir-mmaṇḍayantu* (L. 1) of Photo A.

25. *Ma* :—

(*a*) The Māndā inscription shows the use of the modern form. *Cf.* *muṣaratāḥ* (L. 3).

(*b*) The Kamauli grant shows the use of the Nāgarī or the western variety form.[3]

(*c*) The Torpondighi grant shows the use of the modern form.

(*d*) This is the case also in the Dacca image inscription.

(*e*) The same form is to be found in the Bodh-Gayā inscription of Aśokacalla.

---

[1] *Ibid*, XIX, 33.

[2] *Ibid*, pl. VI, X, 38.

[3] *Ibid*, pl. V, XIX, 34.

(*f*) The Gadādhara temple inscription shows the use of the western variety form.

(*g*) The Cambridge Manuscripts show the use of a slightly archaic form.[1]

26. *Ya* :—

(*a*) The modern form is used in the Māndā inscription in *svepvayā* (L. 3-4).

(*b*) The Kamauli grant shows the use of a cursive form in which the acute angle has not reappeared.[2]

(*c*) The modern angular form is used in the Torpondighi grant.

(*d*) The modern form is also used in the Dacca image inscription in Śri-Nārāyaṇena.

(*e*) The form in the Bodh-Gayā inscription of Aśokacalla is almost the same—the difference being a slight cursiveness.

(*f*) The cursive form from which the acute angle is absent is used in the Gadādhara temple inscription of Gayā.

(*g*) The complete development is shown in the Cambridge Manuscripts.[3]

27. *Ra* :—

(*a*) In the Māndā inscription the archaic arrow-headed form of *Ra* is used.

(*b*) The modern triangular form is used in the Kamauli grant.[4]

(*c*) The same form is used in the Torpondighi grant.

(*d*) This is also the case in the Dacca image inscription.

---

[1] *Ibid*, pl. VI, X, 39.

[2] *Ibid*. pl. V, XIX, 35

[3] *Ibid*, pl. VI, X, 40.

[4] *Ibid*. pl. V, XIX, 36.

(*e*) The form used in the Bodh-Gayā inscription of Aśokacalla is similar but slightly cursive.

(*f*) The western variety form is used in the Gadādhara temple inscription of Gayā.

(*g*) The modern form minus dot is to be found in the Cambridge Manuscripts.[1]

In later periods we find that a slanting cross bar in the interior of *va* denotes *ra* as in modern Assamese :—

(1) Manuscript of Candīdāsa's *Kṛṣṇa-Kīrttana,* fol. 179, *Mallārarāgah* (L. 1).

(2) *Niranta* in L. 4 of the Kāmākhyā minor temple inscription of Śaka 1666=1744 A.D.

28. *La* :—

(*a*) In the Māndā inscription we find two forms of *La.*

(i) The modern Bengali form as in Gopāla (L. 3); and,

(ii) The archaic form in which the base line is still present. *galavāsaḥ* (L. 8).

(*b*) The Kamauli grant shows the use of peculiar 12th century form of *La* which is also found in the Deopārā *praśasti* and the Tetrawan image inscription of the second year of Rāmapāla. The form of this letter is the same as the *Ta* of modern Nāgari.[2]

(*c*) The modern Bengali form is used in the Torpondighi grant.

(*d*) The peculiar *ta*-shaped form is to be found in the Dacca image inscription.

(*e*) This is also the case with the Bodh-Gayā inscription of Aśokacalla.

(*f*) The same form is used in the Gadādhara temple inscription of Gayā.

---

[1] *Ibid*, pl. VI, X, 41.

[2] *Ibid*, pl. V, XIX, 37.

(*g*) The modern Bengali form is to be found in the Cambridge Manuscripts.[1]

The *Ta*-shaped form of *la* still survives in Bengali where a dot is put under *na* to denote *la*.

29. *Va* :—

(*a*) The form used in the Māndā inscription shows that the back of the letter is still cursive and not angular.

(*b*) The same form is to be found in the Kamauli grant.

(*c*) This is also the case in the Torpondighi grant.

(*d*) The same form is to be found in the Dacca image inscription.

(*e*) The Bodh-Gayā inscription of Aśokacalla also shows the same form.

(*f*) This is also the case with the Gadādhara temple inscription of Gayā.

(*g*) The final development is to be found in the form used in the Cambridge Manuscripts.[2]

30. *Śa* :—

(*a*) In the Māndā inscription we have almost the same form of *Śa* as that used in the 11th century records, the difference lying in the curvature of the left limb to the right as in *ga*. *Cf.* *trdaśa* (L. 6).

(*b*) We have a similar form in the Kamauli grant, but here the upper part of the right vertical shows no curvature.[3]

(*c*) The Torpondighi grant shows the use of the 11th century form with a wedge at the lower part of the left limb. *Cf.* *diśi* (L. 9).

---

[1] *Ibid*, Vol. VI, X, 42.

[2] *Ibid*, pl. VI, X, 43.

[3] *Ibid*, pl. V, XIX, 29.

(*d*) The Dacca image inscription shows the use of 11th century form with a short horizontal line instead of a wedge at the bottom of the left limb. *Cf.* *Śrī* (L. 1).

(*e*) The Bodh-Gayā inscription of Aśokacalla shows a short leftward curve at the lower part of the left limb.

(*f*) The same form is to be found in the Gadādhara temple inscription of Gayā, where we notice a shortage in the height of the left limb.

(*g*) We find a transitional form in the Cambridge Manuscripts where we find that the height of the left limb has diminished and we find a separate curve joined to the lower end of it.[1]

This separate curve gradually evolves into two small circles of the modern Bengali. The development of this letter was not complete till the expiry of the 15th century as we find the Cambridge Manuscripts form in the Bengali manuscript of the *Bodhicaryāvatāra*. *Cf.* *śudi* and *śubhaṁ* (L. 3) of fol. 66. The Bengali manuscript of Caṇḍīdāsa's *Kṛṣṇakīrttana* shows the completely developed form for the first time. *Cf.* *ṣolaśata* (L. 6) of fol. 179.

31. *Ṣa* :—

(*a*) The modern Bengali form is used in the Māndā inscription. *Cf.* *muṣarātaḥ* (L. 3).

(*b*) The form of the Kamauli grant is a little more cursive.[2]

(*c*) We find the Bengali form in the Torpondighi grant where the acute angle has not as yet reappeared.

(*d*) The form used in the Dacca image inscription found in the ligature *ṣṭhi* of *pratiṣṭhitetiḥ* (L. 2) is similar to that of the Torpondighi grant.

---

[1] *Ibid*, pl. VI, X, 44.

[2] *Ibid*, pl. V, XIX, 40.

(*e*) The Bodh-Gayā inscription of Aśokacalla shows the use of the western variety form. *Cf.* *teṣāṁ* (L.1).

(*f*) The same form as that of the Bodh-Gayā inscription is to be found in the Gadādhara temple inscription of Gayā.

(*g*) The complete Bengali form is used in the Cambridge Manuscripts.[1] The form used in the Bengali manuscript of the *Kṛṣṇakīrttana* shows that there was no change in subsequent centuries. *Cf.* *Ṣolaśata* (L. 6) of fol. 179.

32. *Sa* :—

(*a*) In the Māndā inscription the wedge in the left limb of the letter is still hollow and open.

(*b*) The form used in the Kamauli grant is peculiar as it shows the suppression of the upper part of the left limb. In the lower part of the same limb we still find the hollow wedge.[2]

(*c*) The hollow open wedge is also to be found in the form used in the Torpondighi grant.

(*d*) The same form is to be found in the Dacca image inscription.

(*e*) The form used in the Bodh-Gayā inscription of Aśokacalla is similar.

(*f*) The same type is used in the Gadādhara temple inscription of Gayā.

(*g*) The Cambridge Manuscripts show the final development of the form of this letter with the solid wedge.[3]

---

[1] *Ibid*, pl. VI, X, 45.

[2] *Ibid*, pl. V, XIX, 41.

[3] *Ibid*, pl. VI, X, 46.

33. *Ha* :—

(*a*) The Māndā inscription shows the transitional form in which it is not yet possible to write the letter at one stroke of the pen. *Cf. tasy-āhaṁ* (L. 4).

(*b*) The Kamauli grant shows the use of the archaic 9th or 10th century form.[1]

(*c*) A transitional form similar to that of the Māndā inscription is to be found in the Bodh-Gayā inscription of Aśokacalla.

(*d*) The form used in the Gadādhara temple inscription is similar.

(*e*) The form used in the Torpondighi grant is the 11th century one, earlier than that of the Deopārā *praśasti*.

(*f*) The form of the Cambridge Manuscripts is also a transitional one, similar to that of the Bodh-Gayā inscription of Aśokacalla and the Gadādhara temple inscription of Gayā.[2]

The development of this letter was not complete even in the middle of the 15th century A.D. as in the Bengali manuscript of *Bodhicaryāvatāra* written in 1435 A.D. we still find this transitional form of *Ha*. The change must have been completed afterwards as the finally developed form is found in the *Kṛṣṇakīrttana* of *Caṇḍidāsa*. *Cf. Hātha* (L. 6) in fol. 179.

---

[1] *Ibid*, pl. V, XIX, 42.

[2] *Ibid*, pl. VI, X, 47.